THE UPSTART GUIDE TO
OWNING AND
MANAGING A
MAIL ORDER BUSINESS

Dan Ramsey

UPSTART PUBLISHING
Specializing in Small Business Publishing
a division of Dearborn Publishing Group, Inc.

Executive Editor: Bobbye Middendorf
Managing Editor: Jack Kiburz
Associate Project Editor: Stephanie C. Schmidt
Cover Design: Paul Perlow Design

Copyright © 1996 by Dan Ramsey

Published by Upstart Publishing Company, Inc.
a division of Dearborn Publishing Group, Inc.

Printed in the United States of America

96 97 98   10 9 8 7 6 5 4 3 2 1

Library of Congress Cataloging-in-Publication Data
Ramsey, Dan.
   The upstart guide to owning and managing a mail order business / by Dan Ramsey.
       p.   cm.
   Includes index.
   ISBN 0-936894-97-0 (pbk.)
   1. Mail-order business—Management—Handbooks, manuals, etc.
   I. Title.
   HF5466.R35   1995
   381'.142'0681—dc20   95-23121
                                                                  CIP

CONTENTS

FOREWORD

by John D. Schulte, Chairman
National Mail Order Association

Mail order, the last frontier for the entrepreneur . . . who, with little more than a burning desire and something to sell, can work hard, build up a good-sized business and perhaps become rich. The beginning of that success comes from specific business knowledge and how it applies to mail order marketing. This book gives you that start. While no one book can give you all the answers to the many facets of mail order marketing, this one will give you the cornerstone on which to build. When you finish this book you will know the general mechanics of operating a mail order business as well as the base knowledge that you must have to succeed in the mail order business. In fact, in virtually any business you may start, to prosper in today's competitive business climate, you will need to learn mail order marketing methods—or know how to hire someone who does. This book will give you the resources you need.

Why mail order?

Mail order and all its related names—direct mail marketing, direct response marketing, database marketing—are "the way" to market product or service. I knew it 14 years ago, Montgomery Ward knew it over 100 years ago. This year you should know it.

During the late eighties, the mail order industry as a whole continued to grow at the rate of nearly *double* that of over-the-counter retail business. In the mid-nineties, mail order is capturing an increasing share of the retail market with no ceiling in sight. The potential for mail order growth in the year 2000 and beyond is unlimited. Not only are consumers searching for more efficient and responsive shopping avenues, mail order marketers are getting more and more precise in their ability to reach the specific people who would most likely be interested in their offer, thanks to the computer. High technology has opened up an entirely new and expanding arena for direct response marketing. Interactive cable TV, the fax machine, the Internet, CD ROM and other technologies will continue to add to the growth and diversity of marketing via mail order. You'll learn about all these technologies in this book.

Another plus for mail order marketers is that the world is fast offering global business opportunities. This worldwide situation puts mail order marketers in the best position to build global market penetration. International mail order success results from today's ease of long distance communication, improved shipping and delivery options, international credit availability and a growing number of international mailing lists. We live in a time of which mail order pioneers only dreamed.

Yes, my friend, you are on to a good thing at a good time. I started on the road to mail order success many years ago by picking up a book. You can start on your road to success in mail order by reading this book. Then continue to learn from the pros, work hard every day, be persistent (empires aren't built in a day) and you can become one of the mail order success stories of tomorrow.

PREFACE

Today's shoppers are too busy to fight the crowds and the clerks. Increasingly, consumers are shopping by mail for clothes, crafts, computers, culinary delights and thousands of other products and services. The mail order business is booming!

And growth means opportunity! Small mail order businesses are arising from the ashes of shopper frustration. Mail order businesses are offering entrepreneurs a balanced way of achieving the American dream with low start-up costs. In fact, you can start your own mail order business at home in your spare time.

However, don't believe that a mail order business is a get-rich-quick venture. It isn't. Like all good things, success in the mail order business requires work. It also offers rewards for creativity. Most important, it offers profits for helping others fill a need.

Are you ready for the challenge?

The Upstart Guide to Owning and Managing a Mail Order Business is a comprehensive look at mail order—which is actually a marketing system rather than a business. Mail order businesses use the proven principles of direct mail marketing.

The Upstart Guide to Owning and Managing a Mail Order Business will guide you through the pitfalls of selecting, starting, owning and managing a successful mail order business. It also explains opportunities on the latest marketing frontier—using technology to increase profits. You'll learn:

- how to select and use computers to efficiently manage your mail order business;
- how to use a computer to market your products and services at lowest cost; and

- how to identify the newest and best computer hardware and software for building your direct mail business.

The Upstart Guide to Owning and Managing a Mail Order Business includes detailed examples from successful mail order ventures. Business and trade terms are defined in context. Specific resources with addresses and phone numbers are included. Each chapter ends with "Action Guidelines," a list of actions you can take to reach your business goals. Also included are charts, worksheets, checklists and examples to help you increase profits while reducing risks.

ACKNOWLEDGMENTS

First things first. Thanks to many people who contributed to the development of this book. They include John Schulte of National Mail Order Association and of Schulte Associates, Patrick Camacho of Patomo Enterprises, Paulette Peach of Direct Marketing Association, Lori Bush-Ziebell of Postalsoft, Bruce Holmes and Michael Sadowski of Haven Corporation, Loren Smith of the United States Postal Service, Ray Melissa of Mailer's Software, Lynn Amaya of Curtis 1000, J. Maggie Best of Entrepreneur Magazine Group, Bobbye Middendorf and Eileen Lawrence of Dearborn/Upstart Publishing, Sydney Baily-Gould of Saxon House Productions, Lori Capps of the Small Business Development Center at Southwest Oregon Community College, The Small Business Administration Office of Business Development, Portland District Office of the Service Corps of Retired Executives, U.S. Department of Commerce's Office of Business Liaison and Minority Business Development Agency, and the U.S. Treasury's Internal Revenue Service. Thanks also to the staff of Communication Solutions.

Business forms in this book were produced using PerFORM Forms Designer for Windows from Delrina Technology Inc.

sion has brought mail order success to QVC and other shopping channels. Interactive cable will soon add more shopping options.

The dramatic expansion of mail order opportunities on the Internet is due to the World Wide Web and Mosaic. The Web is a network of locations or home pages that can be accessed by anyone with Web browser software, such as Mosaic. A home page can view information from a database server connected to the World Wide Web, which offers a voluminous collection of documents ranging from astronomy images, mail-order catalogs and underground poetry to cartoon journals. Someday, your mail order business may be on the Web.

The Mail Order Business Process

Your successful mail order business must have a process. A *process* is simply a series of operations required in making a product or furnishing a service. The process of making a hamburger, for example, requires knowledge (how to prepare), materials (meat, bun, pickle, special sauce), labor (cooking, assembling, packaging) and results in a specific output (a hamburger) in a form that the customer wants.

There is a proven process to producing mail order services. Understanding the mechanics of the process—the required knowledge, materials, labor and expected results—will make you a better and more efficient mail order business manager.

The knowledge required for producing mail order services includes an understanding of business, access to postal regulations, knowledge of printing, understanding of your product or service and a keen awareness of your customers and what they want. In addition, your mail order business will also be more efficient if you have experience managing people or products and knowledge on how to efficiently apply technology to solve business problems.

The materials you will need for mail order services are basic: packaging materials for your product (envelopes, boxes, labels, tape), packaging tools (scales) and marketing materials (ads, product literature, brochures).

Of course, your mail order business will require labor. If your are selling a product by telephone, you will need time and equipment to sell by phone. If you ship a product, you will need labor (yourself or others) to pick (select) and pack the order. In each case, you must understand what the labor requirements of the process are to ensure that the job is being done properly and efficiently.

Finally, you need to define the end result you want. Actually, it is not the final step; it is the first one. Until you understand exactly what your customer requires, you cannot define the other elements in your process: knowledge, materials and labor.

For example, if your customer wants valuable information delivered quickly and accurately, that is the end result you must strive to offer. You cannot efficiently define the components of your process until you have defined your output. In our earlier example, you don't select beef as a material until you've decided that a hamburger is the output or end result you want. You can't make hamburgers using tofu. If you are delivering valuable and timely information, you must also define exactly what your customer wants and how he or she wants it. You can then better decide what knowledge, materials and labor are needed to deliver this output. You must design your process.

All this may sound quite elementary. It is. But it is where more new businesses get lost than anywhere else. They start out with the wrong knowledge, materials and labor for their customers' needs. They look at their solution before they've even discovered what the customer's problem is. They start at the wrong end of the process. This book will guide you in discovering and developing the best—and most profitable—process for your mail order business.

Your Life as a Mail Order Business Owner

What can you expect your life to be like if you decide to start and grow a mail order business? That depends. If you're a square peg trying to fit into a round hole, you will be uncomfortable. If you don't enjoy managing a business and using your skills to help people, you will probably be miserable. If you're looking for a way to get rich quickly, try another line of work—one I haven't discovered yet. But if you enjoy helping other people, you have an understanding of your customers' needs and you have the desire to be an independent business person, owning and managing a mail order business can be a rewarding way of making a living.

One of the greatest advantages of a mail order business is the feeling of independence. Of course, owning a business means that a business also owns you. However, a mail order business can offer you independence from the clock. You can, if you wish, work in the early morning or late at night or on Tuesdays and Fridays. As long as you get your work done, few mail order enterprises require that you be at a specific location at a specific time. And that's what appeals to many who have had nine-to-five jobs for many years.

Another advantage of owning a successful mail order business is that you can share its success with others. You can hire family members and friends as the need arises for office chores, marketing, packing and shipping or other duties. Many small mail order businesses hire children (over age 12) to pick and pack orders after school or on weekends. This job gives young people an opportunity to earn money while they learn how the business world works.

How Mail Order Businesses Make Money

Mail order businesses make money by having a percentage of people order from the mailings sent to them. The percentage of orders needed to make money varies by total mailing costs, the value of the average order and the profit margin. One company may make a profit by having a 1 percent response rate while another may need a 5 percent response rate to be profitable. The big profits in mail order come from building up a satisfied customer base that continues to purchase from you year after year. The first time a person buys from you they are only trying you out. The second time they buy is the most important. In many cases, a mail order business will only break even or possibly lose money on the first sale (ten CDs for a penny, six books for a buck, etc.), knowing that profits will come from future purchases. That's the essence of success for any mail order business.

Income and Profit Potentials

How much can you expect to make operating a mail order business? Of course, much depends on local need, competition, your skills and other factors. But there are some guidelines that will get you started.

First, an established full-time mail order business operated by the owner without employees typically sells about $100,000 to $150,000 in products in a year. Few mail order businesses start out the first year selling that much, but most can do so by the second full year of operation. How much of each sales dollar will you be able to keep?

Of course, much depends on the type of mail order business you establish, your own skills and resources, what you're selling and to whom. Here are some general, very general, guidelines.

A product-oriented business typically spends about half of every dollar on buying and shipping the product (Figure 1.1). Another 35 percent goes for overhead (rent, telephone, advertising, equipment), leaving about 15 percent of each dollar for the owner (including salary and taxes). A mail order business selling something you, yourself, make can also keep a portion (usually about half) of the wholesale value of the product for labor.

A service business that sells by mail keeps more of every dollar. It goes for labor. Overhead expenses eat up about 35 percent of each sales dollar. Direct expenses (shipping, service production cost) take another 15 percent. The remaining 50 percent is yours to keep, after you pay taxes and any supporting labor costs (Figure 1.2, on page 11).

The above percentages are for your second year of operation when you have developed repeat and referral business, have developed a target market and have purchased your equipment and supplies. Your first year will be more difficult as you build your business. During the first year, expect about 75 percent of your estimated income and overhead to be as high as 50 percent of income. That is, if you estimate that second-year sales will total $100,000, estimate first-year sales to be 75 percent of that, or about $75,000. Don't plan on getting rich the first year and you won't be disappointed.

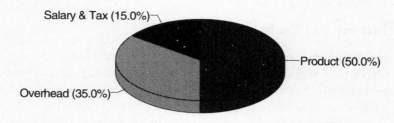

Figure 1.1: Typical expense percentages for mail order products.

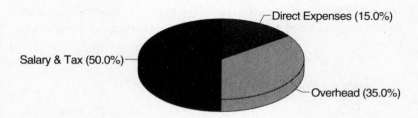

Figure 1.2: Typical expense percentages for mail order services.

Should you add an employee? Only if you are certain that you will increase income by at least *three times* the employee's salary. For example, to hire an employee at $20,000 a year (about $10 an hour), make sure the employee's services will bring you at least $60,000 in business during the coming year. That's a minimum. Some businesses use multipliers of four or even five to determine whether they can afford to hire additional staff. I'll cover finding and hiring good employees later in this book.

Let's take a closer look at overhead expenses. For a typical mail order business you should expect to spend as much as 50 percent of your income the first year and 35 percent in years after that. Where does it go? Rent will be about 10 percent of sales, mailing and office supplies will require another 5 percent and your telephone takes about 10 percent. The remaining 25 percent the first year, and 10 percent in subsequent years, will go for mailing lists, advertising and promotion. The first year's advertising will cost more because you want to get your name out widely and because your advertising won't be as efficient. After the first year of advertising, you'll know which media and messages work best for your market.

These estimates are guidelines to help you in calculating income, expenses and profitability. As your business develops, you may decide to make your salary a higher percentage of sales and reduce the profit or earnings you retain in the business. Or you may decide to reduce overhead expenses by working from your home. Or you may decide to hire a spouse or friend even though it will increase your labor expense. There are many ways you can fine tune your budget. But, to start, stay as close to these percentages as possible. If you spend too little on advertising, for example, your sales may be dramatically reduced because your message isn't reaching your customers.

Understanding the Risks

Certainly, there are many risks involved in starting and running your own business, no matter what type of business it is. But you can minimize these risks by understanding what you're getting into—the purpose of this book—and knowing how to get out of it if you must. Never enter a room without an exit. Chapter 8 will help you discover those exits as well as help you keep from needing them.

A major risk to starting your mail order business is that you will lose your investment of time and money. How can you minimize these risks? Some mail order business owners start their service at home in their spare time while working another job. This structure presents a number of challenges, but they can be overcome. The business can depend on an answering service or a relative to handle phone inquiries. In fact, a mail order business can turn this limitation to an advantage, taking evening and weekend orders by telephone when competitors are closed.

The most successful mail order businesses are those which buy quality mailing lists even though they cost more. The new mail order business can be tempted to buy more names rather than better names. Don't! You'll actually be increasing your financial risks because a poor list will typically net fewer order dollars. For example, renting a quality list may cost $120 per one thousand names but bring you $1200 in business in a month while a $75 per thousand list may only bring you $600 in business each month. Cheap can actually increase risk.

An alternative to high list-rental costs is shared lists. That is, you may be able to trade your list with a noncompeting mail order business. You'll be increasing income while you reduce expenses and risk. I'll cover mailing lists in greater detail in Chapter 3.

The best way to minimize risks is to understand what they are and prepare for those from which you cannot recover. Therefore, you'll want fire insurance. You'll want sufficient operating capital to get you through the first 6 to 12 months of your business. You'll want only minimal office supplies. You'll want to come up with alternative products to ensure that you have income. If possible, make sure that any merchandise or equipment you buy can be returned if your business doesn't work out or can be liquidated with minimal loss. Make sure you have sufficient exits before you enter.

Action Guidelines

This introduction to starting your own mail order business has given you an overview of the business to help you determine if it is right for you. To help you make that decision, following are some actions you can take today:

✔ Start your mail order notebook, writing down ideas and the answers to Action Guideline questions that occur at the end of each chapter.

✔ Check magazines and mail order offers you receive in the mail to see who your competition might be.

✔ Read the mail order offers you receive in the mail and find in magazines to learn who is selling by mail and how they advertise.

✔ Select one or two leading mail order businesses and order something from them. Get on their mailing list. Find out how they treat their customers.

✔ Do some rough calculations of your potential income and expenses based on guidelines in this chapter.

✔ Make a list of the risks you would face by starting your own mail order business.

✔ Talk to others about your ideas to get fresh perspectives on them.

MAIL ORDER BUSINESS REQUIREMENTS

W hat will you need to start and operate a successful mail order business? Certainly you will need a valuable product or service, some money and some customers. But just as necessary is a personal desire to help others. This is important if you are an employee; it is vital if you are the owner. As consumers, we can easily read the attitude of people who serve us. We know when someone is helping us because it's their job or because they enjoy doing their job. And we usually respond by supporting and recommending those who help us solve our problems and make us feel important. They appreciate our business—and they get it.

Before you decide whether operating a mail order business is for you, you must know who *you* are. What do you feel most comfortable doing? Under what conditions do you enjoy working with people? Under what conditions do you prefer to avoid people? What are your personal goals? What are your financial goals? How much risk do you feel comfortable taking? Most important, is a mail order business a good fit in your life or will it cause more problems than it cures? Self-analysis can be difficult, but it is the only way of ensuring that this or any other goal will bring you the results you want in your life.

What Are Your Personal Goals?

Maybe by this stage in your life you've developed a list of personal goals for the next year, five years and beyond. Most people have not.

It isn't mandatory that you develop a long list of your life's goals before you start a mail order or any other business, but it will increase your chances of personal and financial success.

A *goal* is an objective. It is somewhere you want to be or something you want to have. It can be the goal of owning your own mail order business. Or it may be the option of working at home. Or it can be amassing $1 million in assets within 20 years to fund your retirement. Whatever they are, they are your personal goals and they reflect who you are and what you want from your life.

The following are questions to help you determine what you enjoy doing.

- Is there anything that people often compliment you about? A talent, hobby or skill?
- Is there some work or task you would do even if you weren't paid?
- Is there some cause or mission that drives you?
- Is there some opportunity that strikes you as worthwhile?

Colin Matthews loved training horses. He enjoyed working with the individual personalities that horses have to bring out the best in each one. How could he turn this love into a mail order business? Colin designed, wrote and hired a video service to produce tapes on horse training. The video service worked for the cost of tapes and a percentage of sales. The first tape was so successful that Colin now has four tapes available and plans for more. He's doing what he loves.

What Are Your Personal Values?

Values are tools that will take you toward your personal goals. Values are standards or qualities that you've established to help you make daily decisions. Those people who succeed in any business have some common personal values. Let's look at those values together to determine your strengths and opportunities.

Self-Awareness. The process of starting and operating any business is difficult. It will require that you constantly test yourself, maintaining what works and changing what doesn't. But that's what many people love about being a business owner: the endless challenges. It makes them aware of their own personality and skills and requires that they continue to grow.

Hard Work. The great thing about being a full-time independent businessperson is that *you* get to select which *12 hours* of the day you're going to work! It's true. As you start and grow your mail order, you'll spend at least eight hours a day producing your product and another two to six hours marketing and administrating it. Part-time mail order business owners also put in many hours working hard to build their businesses.

Discipline. Discipline is the power behind hard work. You can know exactly what needs to be done and still not do it. Self-discipline forces you to act. Having goals that are meaningful to you will increase your self-discipline.

Independence. Great business owners often make poor employees. They're too independent, which is fine as an owner. They cannot, however, be stubborn. Business owners must maintain a balance between independence and open-mindedness to succeed.

Self-Confidence. It takes a lot of nerve to start a business. It takes a lot more to make it successful. But self-confidence (or nerve) isn't ego. Rather, it's a belief in your unique skills founded on past successes. You know you can successfully operate a mail order business because you have the skills to do so, not just the desire.

Adaptability. Life is chaos. No matter how much we plan, people and events change. Products change. Markets change. We change. A successful business owner must adapt to these changes. Without change, life becomes very dull.

Judgment. To succeed in business, you must make good decisions every day. Wisdom requires knowledge. You must be able to gather complete and accurate facts and make the best decision you can make from those facts. You will not be right every time, but you will be right most of the time. This is good judgment.

Stress Tolerance. Stress has been defined as "the confusion created when one's mind overrides the body's basic desire to clobber some yo-yo who desperately deserves it." Humor can help reduce stress. Stress is a part of everyday life, especially in business. Learning to live with stress without taking it personally can help you succeed in business.

Need To Achieve. Success is the achievement of something you go after. It may be the completion of a project or the start of a business or the learning of a new skill. This need is a driving force within successful business owners that helps give them the energy to reach their goal.

Marilyn Dougherty had trouble finding cosmetics in soft shades that complemented her fair skin. She found one company that had the products she needed, but service was undependable. Their sales literature didn't sell. So Marilyn decided to apply her greatest personal values—self-confidence and discipline—to a new enterprise: Fair Lady Cosmetics. Her mail order venture began on weekends, but now takes much of her time. It also gives her a good income with sales of more than $200,000 a year.

What Are Your Financial Goals?

As much as you may love producing mail order services and helping people, you must also have financial goals. Without a fair salary and profit, you won't be able to help people for very long.

What is an appropriate financial goal for your mail order business? One that funds your other goals. If your business goal is to build a successful mail order business then sell it in ten years and retire, your financial goal must match the expected selling price of your business. If your business goal is to make a good salary as well as a fair return on your investment, you must first determine what a good salary and a fair return mean to you.

One successful mail order business owner established a financial goal of developing annual sales of $150,000 within two years so she could hire her own teenagers. She then wanted to spend three more years building the business to sales of $500,000 or more before selling the business to them and doing some traveling. Her goals were specific and attainable.

What Is Your Risk Tolerance?

Business is legalized gambling. When you start a business you're gambling that you will succeed. You're also facing the risk that you will fail and face personal and financial loss. How much does this risk bother you? How much risk can you tolerate?

Everyone's risk tolerance level is different. Some people cannot afford to lose a dime. Of course, as they say in Las Vegas: "One who can't afford to lose can't afford to gamble." Others say: "I started with nothing. Anything I get is a gain." Still others determine potential losses and say: "It's worth the gamble, but I'm going to do whatever I can to improve the odds."

You must determine your own risk tolerance and that of those with whom you share your life. If you're ready to take the plunge, but your spouse would rather not, find a mutually acceptable level of risk before starting your business. Otherwise, you may find, as too many people have, that you've traded an invaluable relationship for a replaceable business.

A successful mail order operator in the Midwest started with $1,000 in cash. He told himself that once the money was gone, he would close the business. Such a small initial outlay made him very cautious in his business decisions. But it worked. After three years of minimal sales for his part-time venture, he found the right combination. The business began to grow quickly. He then took his initial $1,000 investment out of the business. It was now running on its own financial momentum. He made sure that the most he could ever lose was his initial investment.

Equipment You Will Need

There are a variety of tools available that can make your mail order business more efficient and more profitable. They include mailing equipment, computers, software, printers, copiers, reference books, answering machines, fax machines, desks, chairs and stationery. Here's how successful mail order businesses select these vital tools.

Mailing Equipment

There is a wide variety of equipment available for automating mailing and fulfillment tasks. Most small mail order operators perform these tasks by hand or hire a fulfillment service to fill orders. However, learn as much as you can about mailing and fulfillment equipment by contacting primary suppliers. As your mail order business grows, you'll be ready to take advantage of such systems. Two resources for mailing and fulfillment equipment are included in the next chapter. Contact them to learn what equipment is available, who your local dealers are and how the equipment can reduce expenses for larger mailing operations. Knowing the dealers gives you resources as you have specific questions about mailing and fulfillment.

Copiers

Copy machines can be very useful to your mail order, especially if you don't have a computer and a printer. You will want to conveniently copy correspondence, plans, proposals, contracts, agreements, procedures and other business documents. A good copier can be purchased for under $800. If you're producing your own brochures, direct mail pieces, or other marketing documents, your copy machine can be more cost-effective than running down to the copy shop or printer for a few copies every day.

Features you will want to look for in a copier may include enlargement and reduction, paper trays, collating of multiple copies, and reproduction of photos. Depending on what mail order documents you produce, you may want a copier that can produce duplex or two-sided copies. Or you may want a copier that prints on 11 x 17 inch sheets or one that prints in color. Determine your copying needs before you buy.

Fax Machines

There are more than 25 million fax machines in the world, with most of them installed in businesses. The concept of the fax machine is simple: it reads a sheet of paper for dark spots much like a copy machine does. It then converts these spots into a code that's sent across a telephone line at a speed of nearly 10,000 bits of information per second. Based on international standards, the fax machine on the other end knows how to read these signals and convert them into light and dark spots that conform to the image that was sent. This image is printed on a piece of paper, and you have a facsimile or fax.

The mail order business owner can now send and receive orders, proposals, sales letters, literature, copies of invoices and other printed material to prospects, customers and others in just seconds. A typical one-page fax takes less than a minute to transmit on a Group 3 fax machine, the current standard for facsimile machines. The fax machine, like the computer, is dramatically changing the way that businesses conduct business.

A standard facsimile machine looks like a small printer with a tray to hold outgoing paper and a telephone set either attached or nearby. To send a fax, you call the fax number, your fax machine sends out a tone that tells the other fax machine it would like to transmit a facsimile. The receiving machine sends your machine a high-pitched tone, you manually press your machine's start button and hang up the phone. The fax is being transmitted. Some or all of these processes can be automated depending upon the machine you purchase. In some, you simply put the copy into the machine and press a button that calls a specific telephone in memory; the fax is sent without any outside help.

There are dozens of features to consider when buying a fax machine for your business. However, many are frills. Most important is that your fax machine is Group-3 compatible. Beyond that, explain to the salesperson what you need your fax machine for and let him or her show you the newest features and whistles. You can get a basic fax machine for $300–$400, a better one for $400–$800, and your heart's desire for a thousand dollars or more. Or you can rent or lease a fax machine. This is an especially good idea with equipment like fax machines that quickly become obsolete.

The more expensive fax machines will print on plain paper rather than slick thermal paper that has a tendency to curl and fade. Depending on how you use documents faxed to you and how long you keep them, a plain paper fax may or may not be most economical.

Some fax machines can combine other office functions; by having a standard telephone handset, for example, you can use your fax line for your primary or secondary business line. Some also include a tape or digital answering machine. This setup is practical because your business phone line, feeding into one machine, can serve three purposes: as a regular phone, as a way to receive messages and as a way to take or send faxes. But, like any machine that combines functions, if one goes out or becomes obsolete, they may all go. Compare the cost of a combined unit against the cost of individual units. If there is little difference in total cost, go for the separate components.

If you decide to purchase a computer for your mail order business (see "Computer Hardware" later in this chapter), consider PC fax boards. They are printed circuit boards that are installed inside your computer and allow you to plug in a phone and use it as a fax. There are even models that will serve as your answering machine as well. Fax boards are typically purchased through computer stores. Computer software can let you fax letters, proposals and other documents directly from your computer without printing them first to paper.

Telephone Service

Businesses have a number of telephone service options available to them. The most popular is the 800 number, offered by most long-distance telephone companies. Having an 800 number allows your prospects and customers to call you toll-free. You pay for the call. The advantage is that more people will be inclined to call you. That's also the disadvantage as salespeople will use it to pitch you—on your dime! Toll-free 800 service is available through most long-distance carriers for a small monthly charge plus a per-minute charge that is typically higher than standard long-distance rates. Call your carrier for more information and fees on 800 service: AT&T (800-238-555), Sprint (800-746-3767) or MCI (800-950-5555).

Two new telephone services include 700 service and 500 service. Marketed under various trade names, the 700 service lets calls follow subscribers anywhere within 127 countries and areas. If you work from a variety of offices, a 700-prefix telephone number can be useful. There is typically an enrollment fee and a monthly fee for the service. For more information on 700 service, call AT&T EasyReach at 800-982-8480 or your preferred long-distance carrier.

A 500-prefix telephone number, a new service, automatically routes incoming calls to various locations you select: office, cellular, home, etc. If not picked up at any of the locations, a voice mailbox takes a message from the caller. For more information on 500 service, call AT&T True Connections at 800-870-9222 or your preferred long-distance carrier.

Computer Hardware

A computer is one of the most valuable tools a mail order business can own. It can help you efficiently place orders, track customers, manage inventories, develop sales letters and marketing brochures, and keep track of your income and expenses. You simply cannot operate a competitive mail order business without a computer anymore.

People are often apprehensive about computers because of all the new terminology that they must decipher: CPUs, bits, bytes, bauds, networks, boards, hard disks, RAM, monitor interlacing and so on. Don't worry about it. You'll quickly pick up what the terms mean. Here's a simplified introduction to computers—or it may be a review. As most business computers are IBM-compatible, that's what I'll discuss. Apple's Macintosh computers use a different operating system, but the basics are the same.

CPUs. A CPU is a central processing unit. It is an electronic machine built around a microprocessor called a *chip*, which processes information for you.

The CPU is typically called by the same name as the microprocessor chip that is its brain. Today's PCs (personal computers) use a microprocessor chip called the 486 or the faster 586 (or Intel Pentium microprocessor).

The next number to remember in looking at CPUs is the *clock speed*. Today's microprocessors frequently have clock speeds of 50 MHz (mega or million hertz) and more!

You'll also hear the terms SX and DX. Simplified, a 486DX has more processing power than a 486SX. A DX2 is faster than a DX, and a DX4 is even more so.

So all you really need to know about buying a PC is that a 586, or Pentium, is faster than a 486; a DX4 is faster than a DX2; and a clock speed of 100 MHz is faster than one that's 50 MHz. Fortunately, there's not more than a few hundred dollars difference between fast and super-fast.

Hard Disks. The hard disk drive in your PC can hold thousands of pages of information on some stacked disks (that look like miniature LP records stacked on a record player). The hard disk controller knows where to look for any information you've put into it and it can give you the information in a small fraction of a second.

The storage capacity of a hard disk is measured by the number of bytes or computer (not English) words that it can store. Actually, capacity is normally measured in millions of bytes, or megabytes (Mb). Today's PCs can store 120Mb, 240Mb, 500Mb or a gigabyte (Gb), or more. A gigabyte is *one billion* bytes. To put that in terms that are more understandable, a 1Gb hard disk can theoretically store about a 500,000 typed pages.

RAM. A hard disk is a storage area, much like a library, where millions of pieces of information can be kept. But a computer also needs a work area where files of information can be opened and used. This place is called the *random access memory*, or RAM.

Depending on the size of the programs you will be using, your PC's RAM should be at least 4Mb. Today's PCs typically come with 4 to 32Mb. The larger this work area is, the more work that can be done simultaneously. Some software like Microsoft Windows and Novell NetWare require at least 4Mb and really work better if you have 8Mb of RAM or more.

Diskettes. Data can be moved from one PC to another using small, portable diskettes. These diskettes, sometimes called *floppies*, can store from a third of a megabyte up to nearly one-and-a-half megabytes of information. Once you've developed a file on your hard disk, you can transport the data by instructing the PC to copy it to a diskette.

In the past ten years since PCs have become popular, a number of diskette formats of higher density have evolved. A higher density of magnetic particles allows storage of more information. Early diskettes were 5¼-inches square, and were made of a thin, round, plastic disk placed in a bendable (hence the name floppy) envelope and sealed. Many people have computers that still use these. As technology has developed, however, a greater amount of information can now fit on one diskette. The original diskettes were *single-density*, holding up to 360K (kilo or one thousand bytes), then *double-density* disks stored 720K. *High-density* quickly multiplied storage to 1,200K or 1.2Mb. Many PCs still use the 5¼-inch format.

Another format soon emerged, the 3½-inch diskette with a thin, round, plastic diskette housed in a hard, plastic case. Double-density, 3½-inch diskettes hold 720K, and high-density diskettes store 1.44Mb on a diskette that will fit into a shirt pocket!

The storage capacity of a diskette is a function of the computer as well as the diskette. If you buy a used or older computer, make sure it can read high-density diskettes.

Another option for moving or storing your files is the removable drive. A couple of choices in this area are SyQuest or Bernoulli. They attach to your computer and allow you to place up to 44 or 88Mb of information onto a disk. The disk may be used to back up your data files. This is also an excellent method of storing older files that may be used again, rather than keeping them on your hard drive.

Monitor. To view your computer files, you will need a monitor, similar to a TV screen where the information you're working on is displayed. A monochrome (black and white) monitor is the least expensive. Color monitors are easier to read, and more attractive, but also more expensive. SVGA (super video gate array) monitors are today's cost-effective standard. Rather than get into a boring description of interlacing and pixels, look for a quality monitor that's easy to read. If you can't see the difference between a $300 monitor and one that costs $1,000, don't buy the expensive one. Most monitors require that you buy a separate video card to be installed in the computer. Video cards also have random access memory, called VRAM, to help them display screens quickly.

Printers

Letters and other business documents must be sent from your computer to a printer to be printed on paper. There are many types of printers to select from. But we only need to cover the basics of them here so you'll know which ones to look for.

Dot Matrix. The dot matrix printer forms letters from clusters of dots. A 24-pin printer uses four rows of six pins to form each letter. Today, most dot matrix printers use 24 pins.

Laser. A laser is simply a beam of light that's focused by a mirror. A small laser in your printer actually writes the characters by magnetizing a piece of paper; black dust called *toner* is passed over it and sticks to the places the laser light touched, then the sheet travels through a heater that fuses the black toner to the paper. (Note: An LED, or light-emitting-diode, printer works in virtually the same way.

Bubble Jet. Similar to the laser, the bubble jet printer sprays special ink onto the page in patterns cut by heat. Bubble jet printers are typically less expensive than laser printers.

Which type of printer should you buy? Many small mail order businesses use a dot-matrix printer to produce shipping documents and laser printers for letters and marketing documents.

Software

Now that you understand the basics of computers, you can better see how computer programs work for you. And, even though computer hardware is discussed here first, you will probably select the computer programs or software before you choose the computer or hardware to run it on.

A computer program is a set of instructions written in a language that your computer understands. The program can be as simple as a word processor or as complex as a database. Let's look at the function of each category of computer software.

Operating Systems. DOS stands for disk operating system that comes with your computer and translates commands like "copy" into a language that your PC understands. The most widely used DOS is MS-DOS developed by Microsoft Corp. Novell DOS was developed by Digital Research, now owned by Novell. IBM OS/2 is another popular operating system.

Shell programs make your PC easier to use and perform a number of important maintenance functions. It's called a shell because it wraps around the less-friendly DOS program to make it easier to copy, delete and manage files. Some shell programs also include utilities, or special programs, that help you keep your data organized and safe.

Microsoft Windows, for example, is a shell program that lets you open a number of overlapping boxes or windows on your computer screen, each with different programs in them. If you are writing a letter when a customer calls, you can quickly switch to a window with information about the customer and your current project.

Word Processors. Word processors simply process words. That is, they let you type words into the computer, move them around, insert words, take some out and make any changes you want before you print them to paper. You can use word processors to write letters to customers and prospects. I've used computer word processors for more than ten years and would never go back to typewriters. Word processors let you change your mind.

Common word processing programs include WordPerfect, Microsoft Word, Ami Pro, WordStar and XyWrite. Each has its own unique features and, therefore, a following of loyal users. Some programs are more user-friendly than others. WordPerfect is one of the most widely used word processors. Ami Pro is probably the friendliest. Microsoft Word is popular with users of Microsoft Windows.

Spreadsheets. A spreadsheet arranges numbers into usable form. It's named after the wide multicolumnar sheets that accountants use to make journal entries. There are many ways you will soon find yourself using a spreadsheet software program.

As an example, you can purchase a basic spreadsheet program for about $100 that will let you enter horizontal rows or lines of job expense categories and vertical columns of numbers. Most important, you can then tell the program to make calculations on any or all of the columns or rows and it will do so in less than a second. If you update a number, it automatically recalculates the total for you.

Fancier and more costly spreadsheets can follow instructions you write, called *macros*, to do special calculations automatically. You may want to write a macro that will select all of the invoices over 60 days due and total them up. Better spreadsheets will also produce fancy graphs and pie charts that impress lenders and other financial types.

Popular spreadsheet programs include Lotus 1-2-3, Borland Quattro Pro, and Microsoft Excel.

Databases. A database software program is much like an index card file box. You can write thousands or even millions of pieces of information and store them. But a database program is even better than a file box because it finds information in the files in a fraction of a second.

The most common application of a database program for mail order businesses is a customer file. If you only have a few customers, this may not be necessary. But as you add customers, prospects, and other business contacts, you may soon need at least a simple database program to keep track of them. You can also develop a database of products in inventory, by category.

Your prospect/customer database will keep information such as names, street addresses, cities and states, zip codes, phone and fax numbers, contact names, lists of purchases made, information about buying habits, and even customers' hobbies. Then, if you want to find out how many of your customers are located in a specific city and haven't purchased any services from you last year, you simply tell your database program to search its files for you. It's that easy.

Popular database programs include Borland Paradox, Microsoft Access, Lotus Approach, and Microsoft FoxPro. Depending on which word processor and spreadsheet you select, you may want to purchase a database program by the same company. For example, if you use Lotus's Ami Pro and 1-2-3, consider their database program, Approach. The operating logic of each software developer is slightly different from that of other developers, but you'll usually see continuity within product lines.

Integrated Programs. You can also find integrated software programs that combine the three primary programs: word processor, spreadsheet, and database. Ask your local computer store to recommend a good integrated program. Some also include other related programs, such as communications software that lets your PC talk to other PCs over the phone using modems. The cost of a good quality integrated system is usually much less than the total price for the individual components.

Here's another plus to integrated programs: They talk to each other. That is, your word processor can include financial figures from your spreadsheet in your correspondence and send it by modem to someone listed in your database. Just as important, an integrated group of programs developed by a single software firm will have similar commands in each program. You won't have to learn three separate programs; instead, you'll learn one larger program.

Integrated programs are especially recommended for those who don't want to spend a lot of time selecting and learning numerous software programs. Popular integrated programs include Microsoft Works, ClarisWorks, Lotus SmartSuite, Borland Office, and Microsoft Office.

Vertical Software. In addition to general business programs, there are software programs developed specifically to help mail order businesses. Using such programs will not only make your mail order business more efficient, it can also help you manage your business better as the programs are written specifically to solve problems faced by mail order business owners.

Postalsoft (4439 Mormon Coulee Rd., La Crosse, WI 54601-8231; 800-831-6245) offers numerous computer software programs for increasing mailing efficiency while reducing postage costs. For example, Desktop Mailer assigns ZIP+4 extended ZIP codes, carrier routes and other information to mailing lists, earning postal discounts. Postalsoft also sells database management, document processing and other presort software products. Figures 2.1, on page 29, and 2.2, on page 30, illustrate a presort report produced using the Postalsoft system.

Another popular mail order software program is The Mail Order Wizard (Haven Corp., 1227 Dodge Ave., Evanston, IL 60202-1008; 800-676-0098). The Wizard automates order taking for the small- to medium-sized mail order business. It handles order entry and processing, inventory management, mailing list management and offers numerous reports. The system imports mailing lists, eliminates duplicates, adds ZIP+4 code and POSTNET bar code, prints mailing labels and reports, and performs a variety of other useful mailing functions. The Wizard is modular so you can purchase the components you need for now and add others later as your mail order business grows. A demonstration diskette and guide are available at a small charge.

```
                         PRESORT REPORT

                     Information for Mailer

03/03/95  10:37:59                               C:\DTM\DELIM.MDF


This report summarizes the bulk mail options chosen, postage
computation, and important notes for your information.

You will also need the following reports for this mailing:

    1. The Package List.  Tells how to put mail packages into trays.
    2. PS Form 3602.  The Mailing Statement for the Post Office.
    3. The Required Documentation for Postal Service verification.
    4. PS Form 3553.  The CASS Report (see Note on next page).

You should verify all information below and in the other reports
BEFORE you print labels.  Take all reports to the Post Office
when your present your mailing at the Bulk Mail Acceptance Unit.

DeskTop Mailer version:          3.02 (Feb 23 1995)
Postage table:                   02/09/95

Mailer:                          Your Company Name
                                 Your mailing address
                                 Your city XX   12345

Date - Time:                     03/03/95 - 10:37:59
File:                            C:\DTM\DELIM.MDF
Class:                           Third - Letter
Presort:                         3/5 Digit ZIP+4
                                 Barcoded
Pieces selected for presort:     1849
Presorted according to:          DMM Section M815
Pieces per tray:                 315 minimum, 420 maximum
Weight of piece:                 1.00 oz. (0.0625 lbs.)
Thickness:                       0.050 in./piece

Summary for Entire Mailing:

Category                 Net Rate     Count              Charge
Total 5-Digit Barcoded:    0.166 x      41 pcs. = $       6.806
Total Basic Barcoded:      0.204 x    1792 pcs. = $     365.568
Total Basic:               0.226 x      16 pcs. = $       3.616

Total for Mailing:                    1849 pcs. = $     375.99

Number of pieces with ZIP+4 Barcode:      1833 pcs.
Number of pieces without ZIP+4 Barcode:     16 pcs.
Percent with ZIP+4 Barcode:              99.13 pct.

Post Office of mailing:          123 (MAILING CITY XX)
Processing Category:             Letters
Number of trays:                 7
```

Figure 2.1: Presort report produced by Postalsoft system (page 1).

```
                        Information for Mailer - Page 2

03/03/95  10:37:59                                    C:\DTM\DELIM.MDF

Weight of single piece:            0.0625 pounds (1.00 oz.)
Total weight of mailing:           115.56 pounds
Sacking based on:                  125 pcs.

Total Postage:                     $375.99

Note:
1. You will need to submit Postal Service Form 3553 to certify
that your ZIP+4 addresses were coded by CASS-certified soft-
ware within 1 year (see DMM section A950).  If you used the
Assign Addresses command to get ZIP+4, use the CASS Form
that you printed then.  If you used the USPS or NCOA Export/
Merge, then use the information supplied with your returned
diskettes to manually complete the form.

2. In the Package List, the number of pieces that have
barcodes in a package is the number shown in the "#ZIP+4"
column, provided that the package shows "Bar" in the
Eligibility column.


Form Name: c:\dtm\dot1adr2.frm
Mail label, 1-up, 15/16 x 3-1/2 in., contin. (Avery 4162/4163)
Labels across page:          1     Labels down page:            11
Width of label:          3.500     Height of label:          1.000
Left margin:             0.375     Top margin:               0.000
Width between labels:    0.000     Height between labels:    0.000
Form width:              4.250     Form height:             11.000
Width adjust:            0.000     Height adjust:            0.000
Form type:          Continuous     Orientation:           Portrait
Units:                  Inches

Template Name: bar2.tpl
Barcode below, not for bulk mail, with 2 addr. lines
[FIRST] [LAST]
[COMPANY]
[ADDRESS_1]
[ADDRESS_2]
[CITY] [STATE]  [ZIP]
{Bar}

Printer: HP LaserJet 4/4M on LPT1:
Courier New 10 point

                      - End of Report -
```

Figure 2.2: Presort report produced by Postalsoft system (page 2).

Another resource for vertical software is Mailer's Software (970 Calle Negocio, San Clemente, CA 92673-6201; 800-800-MAIL). Their catalog offers more than two dozen software programs for those who sell and deliver products by mail. Programs are available for operation on DOS and Windows systems as well as on CD-ROM.

AccuMail from Group 1 Software (800-368-5806) has, among other features, a mailing list manager with a mailing list database and standardizer, and a word processor for writing letters.

Mail Order Manager from Dydacomp Development (800-858-3666) is an integrated mail order management program that automates order taking and processing.

What should you look for in a mail order accounting system? Most businesses use separate systems for order entry, invoicing and inventory control. However, mail order businesses often prefer to combine them, especially for smaller mail order ventures. The person taking the order creates the invoice (Figure 2.3, on page 32), packing slip (Figure 2.4, on page 33) and mailing label (Figure 2.5, on page 34) at the same time and adjusts inventory levels as the order is entered. Mail order management programs should also include ZIP code tables and shipping zone codes for United Parcel Service and other carriers to help automate the creation of mailing labels or shipping manifests. They should also produce reports that help users target promotional mailings to specific geographic areas or to customers who have ordered recently. A few mail order programs include general ledger, payables and receivables modules to create an all-in-one system.

Most important, a mail order management system must be fast, reliable and flexible enough to change with the business, and powerful enough to support more and more users without bogging down as the business grows.

Office Supplies

Your mail order business will probably use a wide variety of office and mailing supplies. You will need letterhead stationery and envelopes for general correspondence, mailing envelopes and boxes for product shipments and many other supplies.

Gifts By Mail

Great Gifts for Great Friends

123 Main St.
Yourtown USA
800-555-GIFT

Invoice

Sold to:	Ship to:

Invoice:	Customer No.:	Date:	Sales Rep:
PO No.:	Terms:	Ship Date:	Ship Via:

Product Code	Qty.	Shipped	Description	Price	Total

	Tax	Sales Tax	Total	Amount

Figure 2.3: Mail order invoice.

Gifts By Mail

Great Gifts for Great Friends

**123 Main St.
Yourtown USA
800-555-GIFT**

Packing Slip

Sold to:

Ship to:

Invoice:		Customer No.:	Date:		Sales Rep:
PO No.:	Terms:		Ship Date:		Ship Via:

Product Code	Qty.	Shipped	Description	Price	Total

Tax Rate	Sales Tax	Total	Amount

Figure 2.4: Mail order packing slip.

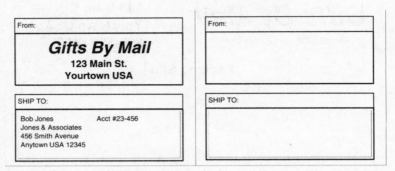

Figure 2.5: Mail order shipping label.

A mail order business, of all enterprises, should buy supplies by mail. Here are some of the larger national office supply providers that sell and deliver by mail: Fidelity (800-328-3034), NEBS (800-225-6380), Office Depot (800-685-8800), Office Max (800-688-6278), Quill Corp. (800-789-5813), Reliable (800-735-4000), Stationery House (800-638-3033) and Viking Office Products (800-421-1222).

Calculating Financial Requirements

How much is all this going to cost? How much money will you need to start your own mail order business? Figure 2.6 (on page 35) will help you make a preliminary estimate of your business's financial requirements. These estimates will be revised and expanded in future chapters.

To estimate start-up costs, you will need to make your best guess of how much it will cost to set up your office for the day you receive your first order. This includes the cost of preparing and equipping your office, getting required licenses and professional memberships, getting the phone hooked up and funding your initial advertising. Assets purchased for start-up can be depreciated and start-up costs can be deducted as legitimate expenses once your business is operating.

Estimating operating costs can be difficult because it requires that you estimate your living expenses as well. Most people who have

Financial Worksheet

Estimated Start-Up Costs:

Office preparation $_____

Office equipment $_____

Initial office supplies $_____

Telephone, answering machine $_____

Utility deposits $_____

ARC and other memberships $_____

Licenses & permits $_____

Insurance and bonds $_____

Professionals $_____

Signs $_____

Initial advertising $_____

Miscellaneous expenses $_____

Total Estimated Start-Up Costs $_____

Estimated Operating Costs:

Living expenses $_____

Employee salaries $_____

Rent $_____

Utilities $_____

Advertising $_____

Insurance $_____

Office supplies $_____

Taxes $_____

Equipment maintenance $_____

Total Estimated Operating Costs $_____

Estimated Financial Resources:

Assets

Checking and savings $_____

CDs and securities $_____

Owed to you $_____

Real estate $_____

Autos and vehicles $_____

Insurance cash value $_____

Other assets $_____

Total assets $_____

Liabilities

Credit cards $_____

Household credit $_____

Auto loans $_____

Taxes $_____

Education loans $_____

Mortgages $_____

Other liabilities $_____

Total liabilities $_____

Total net worth $_____

Figure 2.6: Financial worksheet for calculating your business's start-up and operating costs, and your financial resources.

been employees spend as much as they make; they're not sure exactly what they *need* to live on. However, by starting with your current net (after taxes) salary, you can roughly calculate whether you require more or less to live on. If you operate your business as a sole proprietor (discussed further in Chapter 4), your income taxes and self-employment (Social Security) tax will be paid by the business.

Other operating costs are those expenses that you will pay each month to keep the doors open (fixed or overhead expenses) as well as those that increase as sales increase (variable expenses).

Where can you get the money you need to start your business? A survey of small businesses conducted by Coopers & Lybrand found that 73 percent were funded by the owners and their families, 13 percent by outside investors, 8 percent by banks and 6 percent by alliances with other businesses. However, the survey reported that the businesses that were owner-financed had the highest failure rate. You'll learn how to use your financial resources—and develop new ones—in Chapter 7.

How To Find Products To Sell by Mail

Maybe you already have a product or service in mind that you would like to sell by mail. If not, here's what you should be looking for:

- Unique products that are not found through retailers
- Products that reach a specific market or target group
- Products that are easily packaged and distributed
- Product groups that offer opportunities for additional sales
- Products that can easily overcome competitors
- Products that are easily understood by the buyer

Where should you look for such products? Most large public libraries have a current copy of *Thomas Register of American Manufacturers* (212-290-7225), *McRae's Blue Book* (212-673-4700) and other industrial guides. These guides offer contact information for manufacturers of a wide variety of products. Some will have unique products you can sell by mail while others will produce products from your design. A few will drop-ship products directly to your customers. In addition, the NMOA (see Chapter 3) is a good source for finding products. They publish information on new products in *Mail Order Digest.*

How To Manage Your Time

How can the mail order businessperson ensure that time is well managed? Here are a few ideas offered by successful business people.

First, organize your work space so that important papers don't get lost and unimportant papers do. You can also make a rule that you will avoid handling papers more than once. If you pick up a piece paper, make a decision regarding it right then if possible.

Second, set up a regular work schedule. It may be from 7 A.M. to 6 P.M., or 8 A.M. to 5 P.M., or 6 A.M. to 6 P.M. Whatever it is, try to stick to it. If you manage your time well, you will be able to. If you have one time of the day that seems more productive for you than others, plan your most important functions around it.

Third, take advantage of otherwise wasted travel and unproductive time. Take work with you in a briefcase or purchase a laptop computer that you can use to keep productive every minute. As your time management skills improve you'll learn how to do more than one thing at a time. You could be making job notes or talking with a key employee or gathering information on an upcoming project while you're waiting to talk with a customer.

Meetings seem to be one of the biggest time-wasters. But you can change this by carefully preparing for all of your meetings. Meetings, to be productive, must have a purpose or agenda and a time limit. Even if you didn't call the meeting, if you see that it has no focus or structure, you can step in and say, "I have another appointment in an hour. What topics do we have to cover in that hour?" Then list those topics as the agenda.

Finally, use one of the popular time management planning systems to help you get the most out of your day. They include Day Timer (Day Timers, Inc., One Day-Timer Plaza, Allentown, PA 18195-1551; 800-225-5005), Day Runner (Harper House, Inc., available through most stationery stores) and Planner Pad (Planner Pads, Inc., 5088 S. 107th St., Omaha, NE 68127; 402-592-0666). These and other systems give you a place to record appointments, daily to-do lists, special projects and their steps, as well as a contact book for names and addresses. If you spend most of your time in the office at a computer, there are numerous contact management and scheduling programs that will help you manage your time. If you use a portable computer, you can install these programs and carry this information wherever you go.

Time and stress are closely related. The lack of time to do what you need to do often increases personal stress. How do you manage both? Following are some ideas from a successful mail order business owner:

- Plan your time and establish priorities on a daily to-do list.

- Decide what your prime time is and do your most important or difficult tasks then.

- Set business hours, specific times when you're at work and times when you turn on the answering machine because you're on duty but off call. You, your customers and your family will appreciate knowing your set routine, even though you know that for special events or emergencies you can break that schedule.

- Confirm your appointments one-half day before the appointment—afternoon for next morning or morning for that afternoon. It will save you time, and your customers will appreciate the consideration.

- If you're working from your home, give your business as much of a separate and distinct identity as possible. Although you might save a few dollars by using the dining room table as a desk and a cardboard box as a file cabinet, the stress and strain of operating without proper space and supplies will take its toll.

- Have a separate room or area for your business, with a separate entrance if customers visit. Consider soundproofing so your family won't be bothered by your noise and vice versa. In addition to the psychological and physical comfort of having a separate room for your home office, the IRS requires it in order for you to make a legitimate claim for tax deductions.

Action Guidelines

You've learned the requirements of starting and operating a successful mail order business. They include evaluating your personal and financial goals as well as your tolerance for risk, reviewing the tools you need, calculating financial requirements, assessing the skills you will need to be successful and learning how to efficiently manage your time. Here's how to implement what you've learned in this chapter.

✔ Using your mail order business notebook, make notes regarding your personal goals and values, your financial goals and your tolerance for risk. Be as honest as possible.

✔ Plan your purchase of a computer, printer and software for your mail order business. Don't buy it yet; just start learning what you can about them.

✔ Complete the financial worksheet in this chapter to determine how much you'll need and where you can get it.

✔ List the skills you'll need to enhance or add to make your mail order business successful. How can you develop or improve on these skills?

✔ Select and use a time-management system if you don't already.

✔ Review your mail order business requirements and start thinking about resources, the topic of the next chapter.

Chapter

3

RESOURCES FOR YOUR MAIL ORDER BUSINESS

A resource is a person, product or service that can help you with your objectives. Resources for your mail order business include your own experiences, your prospective customers, trade associations, conventions, seminars, training courses, books, magazines and governmental services. Together they can increase your working knowledge of mail order as well as help you understand how to work efficiently and profitably.

This chapter offers information on these and other resources. Included are addresses and telephone numbers when appropriate to help you get your mail order business off the ground.

Your Own Experiences Buying by Mail

The first and most important resource for your mail order business is you. Your experiences with mail order services may be limited to occasionally buying personal products by mail. Or you may have experience in retail or direct mail sales. Or maybe you don't have extensive experience with mail order sales, but you do have extensive knowledge of the products you want to sell by mail.

The point is that to serve your customers well you must understand their needs. You must know how they feel, what they need, how and what they buy. The best experience you can have is to work for a successful mail order business. Next is to have other retail business experience or have purchased many products by mail.

Take time to review your own experiences with mail order. Think of yourself as a mail order customer as you answer these questions:

- What have you purchased by mail in the past?
- Were there any specific mail order purchases that were especially easy or problematic?
- What products have you or would you buy by mail? Why?
- When buying by mail, what do you feel are the most important factors in selecting a mail order supplier?
- What experiences in mail order buying have made you want to buy more? Stop buying?
- List five or six features that, in your experience, must be offered by a mail order business.

In any business, success requires empathy and empathy requires experience. The more you understand about your customer, the better you will be able to serve him or her.

Researching Customer Needs

The best way to understand your customers is to interview them. Find out what they are thinking. Understand what they want from a mail order business and from you. Ask them what is most important to them. Learn what makes them select one mail order business over another.

How can you find out what customers want before you start your mail order business? By interviewing prospective customers. Talk with friends who have recently purchased products or services by mail. Set up a part-time mail order business, and on evenings or weekends, interview people who order from you.

In general, you'll learn that your customers want an effective mail order business that offers service and satisfaction. Depending on your chosen clientele, the next most important requirement may be price, speed or quality. They may want to buy at the guaranteed lowest price or need to receive merchandise within 24 hours or desire a company that will offer credit terms. You may learn that two of these three elements—price, speed, quality—are already served by mail order retailers in your field and that there is a sufficiently large market for another mail order business that offers the third element.

Chapter 6 will cover marketing in greater detail. For now, work toward an understanding of your potential customers' needs.

Mail Order Trade Associations

A trade association is a group of businesses that agree to share information among themselves regarding their trade. Plumbers have them, car makers have them; so do mail order business owners.

A major trade association for this profession is the Direct Marketing Association (Membership: 6 E. 43rd St., New York, NY 10017-4646; 212-768-7277, ext. 385). DMA membership is open to businesses that use or sell direct mail and direct response advertising services. It promotes direct mail interests to legislators, sponsors seminars and trade conventions, publishes trade journals and newsletters, and arbitrates disputes. Annual dues start at $750.

Another leading trade association is the National Mail Order Association (2807 Polk St. NE, Minneapolis, MN 55418-2954; 612-788-1673). Aimed at small- and medium-sized mail order companies, the NMOA was formed in 1972 and now has members around the world. Dues are less than $100 a year for North American members and slightly more for international members to help cover the higher cost of mailing overseas. NMOA also offers a bulletin board service that members can access to share information with other members.

The Advertising Mail Marketing Association (1333 F St., Suite 710, Washington, DC 20004-1108; 202-347-0055) represents direct marketers, mailing industry suppliers and others interested in advertising mail or postal issues.

There are many other trade associations for mail order and direct mail businesses, including:

- American Association of Home-Based Businesses (301-963-9153).
- American Home Business Association (801-273-5450).

- Home Office Association of America (212-980-4622).
- National Federation of Independent Businesses (800-634-2669).
- National Home Office Association (800-664-6462).

Mail Order Conventions and Seminars

Many professional associations and marketing groups sponsor annual conventions of members and professionals. Workshops, guest speakers and roundtables are organized to encourage mail order business owners from across the country to share information, techniques and ideas.

Direct Marketing Association (see above) seminars include "Basic Institute," "Beyond the Basics," "Database Marketing," "Fulfillment and Customer Service Excellence," "Profitable and Effective Use of the Telephone," "The Law and Direct Marketing," "Winning Direct Mail" and others. Seminars, held in various metropolitan areas, are open to DMA members and nonmembers.

Here's another useful resource for direct mailers. The National Direct Mail Archives (401 N. Broad St., 5th Floor, Philadelphia, PA 19108; 800-777-8074) publishes an informative newsletter called *Who's Mailing What!* It reports on what direct mail packages are being mailed across the nation and how they're doing. It's a relatively low-cost way to watch and learn from your competition.

Books on Mail Order

There are numerous intermediate and advanced books on mail order and direct mail methods. The most popular is *Successful Direct Marketing Methods, 5th Edition* by Bob Stone (NTC Business Books, 1994; 800-435-2937). Other valuable reference books include: *Creative Strategy in Direct Marketing* by Susan K. Jones (NTC Business Books, 1991; 800-435-2937) and *The Golden Mailbox* by Ted Nicholas (Dearborn, 1992; 800-829-7934).

In addition, the DMA offers reference books on mail order and related topics that are published by others. They include *Direct Mail and Mail Order Handbook* and *The Greatest Direct Mail Sales Letters of All Time*, both by Richard Hodgson; *Direct Marketing Manual,*

DMA Annual Report, DMA Directory of Membership and *Fact Book on Direct Marketing* among others.

The following books are available through Mailer's Software (800-800-MAIL): *Common Sense Direct Marketing, Insider's Guide to Demographic Know-How, Official Mail Management Guide, Direct Marketing Strategies and Tactics, Profitable Direct Marketing* and others.

In addition, most popular books on mail order are available from the National Mail Order Association (612-788-1673) with discounts offered to NMOA members.

Upstart Publishing (800-829-7934) offers numerous books for those wanting to start or expand their small business.

Magazines and Trade Journals

Monthly magazines and trade journals will help you keep up on what's new in your trade. They inform you of pending postal legislation, conventions and seminars, new ideas and methods, as well as advertise services.

Trade journals for the mail order business include *Council Newsletter, Dateline: DMA, Direct Line, DMA Washington Report* and others published by the Direct Marketing Association (see above). The National Mail Order Association (see above) publishes *Mail Order Digest* and *Washington Newsletter*, both monthlies. Other trade journals include *AMMA Bulletin* (202-347-0055), *Direct Marketing* (516-746-6700), *DM News* (212-741-2095) and *Memo to Mailers* (USPS National Customer Support Center, 6060 Primacy Pkwy., Suite 101, Memphis, TN 38188-0001).

Mail Order Business Opportunities

You can learn from others by purchasing a business opportunity or a franchise. A business opportunity allows you to sell a product or service without the strict requirements of a franchise. Depending on the opportunity, you may be licensed to use the name of whomever you purchased the business opportunity from in your advertisement.

Another way of learning from others is to become an agent of a specific supplier. A supplier will furnish you with a product that you can then resell to your customers. Depending on how large of a customer you are, the supplier may help you with advertising or marketing, pass along prospects or even supply product on consignment. Some suppliers will drop-ship product. That is, once you have an order, you send the wholesale price and a shipping label to the supplier who forwards the product on to your customer.

Franchising is a form of licensing by which the owner (the franchisor) of a product or service distributes through affiliated dealers (the franchisees). The franchise license is typically for a specific geographical area. The product or service is marketed by a brand name (McDonalds, Sears), and the franchisor controls the way that it is marketed. The franchisor requires consistency among the franchisees through the use of standardized products or services, trademarks, uniform symbols, equipment and storefronts. The franchisor typically offers assistance in organizing, training, merchandising and management. In exchange, the franchisor receives initial franchise fees and an ongoing fee based on sales levels.

One useful source of information on available franchises is the *Franchise Opportunities Handbook* produced and published by the United States Department of Commerce and available through the Superintendent of Documents (U.S. Government Printing Office, Washington, DC 20402) or your regional federal bookstore. This handbook lists basic information on franchises available in 44 categories including the name and address of the franchisor, a description of the operation, number of franchises, how long the franchise has been in business, how much equity capital is needed, how much financial assistance is available, what training is provided and what managerial assistance is available.

Another source of information on franchises is the International Franchise Association (1350 New York Avenue N.W., Suite 900, Washington, DC 20005). The IFA's *Franchise Opportunities Guide* is a comprehensive listing of franchisors by industry and business category. *Franchising Opportunities* is their bimonthly magazine. Their newsletter, *Franchising World,* includes information on developing trends in franchising.

Other sources include *Entrepreneur, Income Opportunities* and other magazines available on most newsstands.

List Sources

There are two types of mailing lists: compiled and response. Compiled lists are derived from directories, telephone books, association membership rosters, government sources and public records. Response lists are of individuals who responded to advertising or requested more information. Mailing list sources include:

- AccuData America (1326 Cape Coral Pkwy, Cape Coral, FL 33904-9607; 800-732-9250)

- Allmedia International (4965 Preston Park Blvd., Suite 300, Plano, TX 75093; 800-466-4061)

- Best Mailing Lists (888 S. Craycroft Rd., Tucson, AZ 85771; 800-692-2378)

- Cahners Direct Marketing Services (1350 E. Touhy Ave., Des Plaines, IL 60018; 800-323-4958)

- Contacts Influential (1001 SW 5th Ave., Suite 1000, Portland, OR 97204-1175; 503-227-1900)

- Customized Mailing Lists (1906 Field Rd., Sarasota, FL 34231; 800-237-LIST)

- Database America (100 Paragon Dr., Montvale, NJ 97645; 800-223-7777)

- Dunhill International List (1951 NW 19th St., Boca Raton, FL 33431; 800-DUNHILL)

- Marketry (2020 116th Ave. NE, Suite 100, Bellevue, WA 98004; 800-346-2013)

- PCS Mailing List Co. (85 Constitution Ln., Danvers, MA 01923; 800-532-LIST)

- TRW Business Marketing Services (505 City Parkway W., Orange, CA 92668; 800-432-4292)

How much will you pay for a mailing list? The typical charge is between $50 and $100 per 1,000 names for one-time use. You can purchase directly from the list owner or work through a list broker who will charge a commission to the list owner. A list of direct mail resources is available in the *Directory of Mailing List Companies*

(Todd Publications, 18 N. Greenbush Rd., West Nyack, NY 10994; 914-358-6213).

Media Resources

Which advertising media you use to promote your mail order product or service depends on what you're selling and to whom. Advertising rates for magazines, card decks and other media are published in directories available from Standard Rate and Data Service (3004 Glenview Rd., Wilmette, IL 60091; 800-851-7737) or through many larger public libraries.

Packets of postcard-size direct-mail pieces—called card decks—are published by the following companies, among others:

- Cutting Edge Opportunities Deck (1250 Ridge Rd., Elizabethtown, PA 17022; 800-348-4460)
- Dartnell (4660 N. Ravenswood Ave., Chicago, IL 60640; 800-621-5463)
- Doyle Publishing (2101 Rexford Rd., Charlotte, NC 28211; 704-364-0719)
- Exec-Cards (211 State St., Rockford, IL 61105; 800-435-2937)
- Hughes Communications (211 W. State St., Rockford, IL; 800-435-2937)
- Venture Communications (60 Madison Ave., New York, NY 10010; 212-684-4800)

Equipment Suppliers

Two leading suppliers of mailing and fulfillment equipment are Friden Neopost and Pitney Bowes. Friden Neopost (800-624-7892) markets mailing and fulfillment equipment. Pitney Bowes (800-672-6937) makes postage meters and related mailing equipment. Check your regional telephone book under "Mailing Machines & Equipment" for a list of local equipment suppliers.

Postal Service Resources

The United States Postal Service operates more like a business than nearly any other component of the federal government. As such, it does whatever it can to encourage the sales of postal services. That means the USPS helps mail order businesses plan and deliver direct mail. They can help you.

The USPS handles over 580 million pieces of mail every day. Much of it is from or to businesses. For more information on efficiently using postal services, call their Customer Service Center at 800-222-1811, or write to USPS Marketing Department, P.O. Box 2484, Warminster, PA 18974-0049. Ask for a complimentary copy of *Postal Business Companion,* which describes postal services, explains mailing lists and mail preparation, and defines postal terms and abbreviations. It also includes information on telephone area codes, time zones and common business terms.

First-class mail is used for sending correspondence, postcards, bills, statements of account and checks which weigh less than 11 ounces. First-class mail above 11 ounces is called Priority Mail. A 3-ounce letter costs 78 cents to mail domestically. First-class mail in quantities greater than 500 earn a lower bulk rate if you follow regulations and have a bulk-rate permit.

Second-class mail is a special mailing class for publishers of newspapers, magazines and other periodicals.

Third-class mail is printed matter under 1 pound that earns a lower rate. A 3-ounce envelope can be mailed for 78 cents, the same as that for first-class. Third-class bulk rates are available when at least 200 pieces (or 50 pounds) are mailed at the same time under standardized requirements.

Fourth-class mail rates are available for shipping bound printed material such as books. The rate depends on the weight in pounds and the zone. For example, a 3-pound package can be mailed across the country (zone 8) for $2.45. A fourth-class bulk rate discount is also available if more than 300 pieces are mailed at the same time.

As of January 1, 1995, the USPS has new postal rates. A current postal rate and information chart is available from the USPS or from Curtis 1000 (800-766-1007). Here's a summary for comparison:

	1st Oz.	Additional Oz.
First-class	0.32	0.23
First-class/discounted		
Nonpresorted	0.305	0.23
Barcoded	0.295	0.23
Presorted*	0.228	0.23
Carrier route*	0.208	0.23
ZIP+4 presorted*	0.221	0.23
5-digit barcoded*	0.212	0.23
Third-class (letters)	Less than 3.3071 oz. each	
Basic sorting	0.226	
Basic ZIP+4	0.216	
Basic barcoded	0.204	
Fourth-class (books)	Local	Zone 8
Not over 2 pounds	1.12	2.10
Not over 5 pounds	1.22	2.14
Not over 10 pounds	1.37	4.87

* =More than 2 oz., 500 minimum per mailing

Common mailing rates cover four pages of small print so the above numbers are for comparison only. Contact the USPS for complete information, rates and requirements.

The USPS offers a number of publications to help you learn more about postal rates and regulations. They include:

- *Addressing for Success* (Notice 221).
- *Designing Letter Mail for Postal Automation* (Publication 25)
- *Postal Addressing Standards* (Publication 28)

These and others are available through most local post offices. In addition, the following publications can be ordered through the Superintendent of Documents (U.S. Government Printing Office, 941 N. Capital St. NW, Washington, DC 20402-9375):

- *Domestic Mail Manual*
- *National ZIP Code Directory*
- *Postal Bulletin*

Fulfillment Houses and Lettershops

To reduce start-up costs, you can use the services of fulfillment houses, inbound call centers and lettershops for taking and fulfilling orders. You'll find such services advertised in trade publications (see above) as well as in your local telephone book under "Mailing Services."

A fulfillment or inbound call center will charge a one-time setup fee, a per-call processing fee, a monthly minimum, as well as fees for special transactions such as payment processing or special fulfillment.

Federal Trade Commission Resources

The Federal Trade Commission (FTC) was established to prevent unfair and deceptive trade practices. To do this, it has developed numerous regulations. The Mail Order Rule became effective in 1976 in response to customer complaints about mail order businesses that didn't ship goods on time. To comply with this rule, simply ship goods within the time stated in your ads or no later than 30 days after receiving the order.

If you're unable to ship merchandise on time, you are required to send a written notice advising the customer by first-class mail that they can consent to the delay or may cancel the order and receive a prompt refund. All refunds must be sent by first-class mail within seven days of the order's cancellation. If payment was made by credit card, you must make refunds within one billing cycle after the order is canceled.

That being said, a successful mail order business will go beyond the requirements of law to ensure that the customer is treated fairly. Most successful mail order businesses ship merchandise within three business days of receiving the order. If any items are back ordered, the mail order business will immediately notify the customer which items are not being shipped, when they will be shipped, and offer to cancel the order or a portion if the customer is not satisfied. This "golden rule" has turned mail order from a last choice to a first choice for many purchasers.

Additional information on the Mail Order Rule and related topics for mail order businesses is available from the Federal Trade Commission (Pennsylvania Ave. at 6th St. NW, Washington, DC 20580; 202-326-2222).

Small Business Administration Resources

It was Will Rogers who said "Be thankful we're not getting all the government we're paying for." Small business owners can get some of their money back by using the assistance of the federal and state governments to help them succeed in business.

Founded more than 40 years ago, the U.S. Small Business Administration or SBA (1441 L Street N.W., Washington, DC 20416) has offices in 100 cities across the U.S. and a charter to help small businesses start and grow. The SBA offers counseling, booklets on business topics and administers a small business loan guarantee program. To find your area's SBA office, check the white pages of metropolitan telephone books in your region under "United States Government, Small Business Administration."

The SBA also operates the Small Business Answer Desk, a toll-free response line (800-827-5722) that answers questions about SBA services. In addition, it sponsors the 13,000 Service Corps of Retired Executives (SCORE) volunteers, Active Corps of Executives (ACE) volunteers, Small Business Development Centers (SBDC), and Technology Access Centers (TAC).

The SBA offers numerous publications, services and videos for starting and managing small businesses. Publications are available on products/ideas/inventions, financial management, management and planning, marketing, crime prevention, personnel management and other topics. The booklets can be purchased for one or two dollars each at SBA offices or from SBA Publications, P.O. Box 30, Denver,

CO 80201. Ask first for SBA Form 115A, *The Small Business Directory*, that lists available publications and includes an order form.

Another popular service is SBA On-Line, a computer bulletin board operated by the Small Business Administration. It receives more than 1,000 calls a day and has handled one million calls since it opened in 1992. Once you're familiar with computers and modems, you can access this resource by having your system call 900-463-4636. There is a small fee for its use, currently about $6 an hour. The bulletin board includes extensive resources for small businesses and access to other government agencies. If you want to access a limited version of this popular bulletin board, dial 800-697-4636. It doesn't have as many resources, but it is free.

If you're already using the Internet, SBA On-Line can also be accessed through the World Wide Web (WWW). Their address is http://www.sbaonline.sba.gov. For technical help or more information, call 202-205-6400.

The Service Corps of Retired Executives (SCORE; 1441 L Street N.W./Room 100, Washington, DC 20416) is a national nonprofit association with a goal of helping small business. SCORE is sponsored by the SBA and the local office is usually in or near that of the local SBA office. SCORE members, retired men and women, and ACE members still active in their own businesses donate their time and experience to counseling individuals regarding small business.

The 700 Small Business Development Centers (SBDCs) are regional centers funded by the SBA and managed in conjunction with regional colleges. An SBDC offers free and confidential counseling for small business owners and managers, new businesses, home-based businesses and people with ideas concerning retail, service, wholesale, manufacturing and farm businesses. SBDCs sponsor seminars on various business topics, assist in developing business and marketing plans, inform entrepreneurs of employer requirements and teach cash flow budgeting and management. SBDCs also gather information sources, assist in locating business resources and make referrals.

Small Business Institutes are partnerships between the SBA and nearly 500 colleges offering counseling services to area businesses. SBIs conduct market research, develop business and marketing plans, and help small businesses work out manufacturing problems. Contact your regional SBA office to find out if a local college has such a program. You could get free or low-cost assistance from the college's business faculty and students.

Tax Information Resources

The U.S. Treasury Department's Internal Revenue Service offers numerous Small Business Tax Education Program videos through their regional offices. Topics include depreciation, business use of your home, employment taxes, excise taxes, starting a business, sole proprietorships, partnerships, self-employed retirement plans, Sub-Chapter S corporations and federal tax deposits.

If you're considering using a portion of your home as a business office, request *Business Use of Your Home* (Publication 587) from the Internal Revenue Service (Washington, DC 20224). It's free and will help you determine if your business qualifies for this option as well as how to take advantage of it to lower your taxes. If so, you will add Form 8829, *Expenses for Business Use of Your Home*, to the sheaf of forms you file with your Form 1040 and Schedule C.

Depending on how much you use your business vehicle for personal use, you can either list all costs of operating the vehicle as an expense or you can deduct a standard mileage rate as an expense when you file income taxes. For more information, request *Business Use of a Car* (Publication 917) from the Internal Revenue Service. There's no charge for this publication. Figure 3.1, (on page 54) can help you keep track of auto mileage and expenses on behalf of your mail order business.

What business expenses are deductible? There's a long list. The best answer is found in a free publication offered by the Internal Revenue Service, *Business Expenses* (Publication 535).

To begin your payroll system, contact the Internal Revenue Service (Washington, DC 20224) and request the *Employer's Tax Guide* (Circular E) and get a nine-digit Employer Identification Number. The IRS will then send you deposit slips (Form 8109) with your new ID number printed on them. Use these deposit slips each time you pay your payroll taxes. Payroll taxes are paid within a month of the ending of a quarter; that is, January 31, April 30, July 31 and October 31. As your business grows, you may be required to pay payroll taxes more frequently. By then, your accountant will help you determine need and the process.

Gifts By Mail
Great Gifts for Great Friends

123 Main St.
Yourtown USA
800-555-GIFT

Automobile Travel Log

Date: _____

Monthly Summary Sheet

_____

AUTOMOBILE INFORMATION

Make of Auto: _____

Year & Model: _____

Vehicle I.D. Number: _____

Driver of Vehicle: _____

Odometer reading: End of month: _____

                    Beginning of month: _____

Total Miles Driven: _____

Qualified Business Miles Driven: _____

Allowable Reimbursement Rate: _____ x $_____ /mile

Total Expense   _____

YEAR TO DATE - INFORMATION

	BUSINESS MILES	TOTAL MILES
Prior YTD	_____	_____
Current Month	_____	_____
New YTD	_____	_____

DATE: _____

SIGNATURE : _____

APPROVAL : _____

Figure 3.1: Automotive mileage driven for business purposes is a legitimate expense. Keep track of mileage with a travel log.

Action Guidelines

There is a wide variety of resources available to mail order business owners including your experiences, prospective customers, trade associations, conventions, seminars, books, magazines, suppliers and governmental offices. Here's how to put them to work for you:

✔ Review your own experiences with mail order services as well as the experiences of friends and family.

✔ Make notes in your mail order notebook on what you feel your prospective customers need and want from a mail order business.

✔ Start calling and writing for catalogs and information from resources.

✔ Review your list of skills and needs, then find training resources to enhance them.

✔ Contact suppliers, business opportunities and franchisors to determine costs and benefits of using their knowledge to start your mail order business.

✔ Contact your regional SBA and SBDC offices to learn how they can help you start and build your business.

✔ Contact the IRS for booklets, forms and other resources.

Chapter

4

STARTING UP YOUR MAIL ORDER BUSINESS

By now, you've learned what a successful mail order business does, studied the resources available to you and decided that you want to start your own mail order. You're ready to direct market your first product and find your first customer, right?

Not yet. Before you start your mail order business, you must first plan to make it a success. You don't want to close up shop in six months because you misjudged the market or overspent your income. Instead, you want to celebrate your first anniversary looking back on a successful year and looking forward to many more.

This chapter will help you plan for your success, then execute that plan to ensure that your mail order business will be profitable.

Planning To Succeed

The adage that businesses don't plan to fail, they just fail to plan is accurate. Without a plan for your business, you may soon find yourself in a venture that neither satisfies your needs nor pays your bills.

A business plan is a document that can be used both by people contemplating going into business and those already in business. A business plan helps you focus your thoughts and ideas, summarizing your product, your process, your market and your expectations into a single document that can guide you in your daily decisions as well as help you develop financing for start-up and expansion.

An excellent guide for creating a successful business plan is David

H. Bangs, Jr.'s best-seller *The Business Planning Guide, Sixth Edition* (Upstart Publishing). It offers clear, step-by-step procedures for pulling a business plan together for a mail order business or any other business venture. It includes worksheets, resources and a sample business plan.

Your business plan will answer these five questions:

1. How much money do I need?
2. On what will the money be spent?
3. Who will own and who will operate the business?
4. What are the projected financial results of the business?
5. Do I really know enough about this business?

If your business plan is intended to develop financing through a bank or a backer, it must also answer the question: How will the funds be repaid?

Your business plan will include a statement of purpose, an outline of your product or service, a discussion of your customers and how you will reach them, as well as current and projected financial information.

A typical mail order business may develop a statement of purpose that reads:

ABC Uniforms-by-Mail will offer a wide variety of professional uniforms in all sizes at reasonable prices. Start-up requires $10,000 in cash from savings for inventory, equipment, supplies and a salary for the first two months of operation until the business is expected to be profitable.

If you're using the business plan to develop financing, it will be more developed and specific than the plan you would write to guide you through the first year of operation. In addition, a business plan for a $10,000 start-up is typically shorter than one for a $100,000 expansion project.

A successful business plan will include the following information, as appropriate to your business:

- Description of your business and a statement of its purpose

- Table of contents of your business plan

- Description of the services or products your business will provide

- Information on the location of your business and, if necessary, plans for expansion of the physical plant

- Definition of the management of the business, job descriptions and qualifications

- List of personnel who will initially be employed

- Description of your business's marketing plan

- Information on your competition and market share

- Outline of your price structure and the philosophy behind it

- Facts on short- and long-term trends in the market

- Discussion of quality and how you expect to obtain and retain it in your business

- Description of the sources and requirements of funds including inside and outside investors, and their participation in your business

- A capital equipment and capital improvement list

- An opening balance sheet for your business

- A breakeven analysis for your business

- Monthly income projections for the first three years of business

- A list of the independent professionals hired to assist you in the establishment and management of your business, such as accountants, attorneys, financial consultants, etc.

Writing a Marketing Plan

A marketing plan is simply a description of how you plan to market or develop customers for your mail order business. You can incorporate your marketing plan into your business plan or you can make it a separate document. That decision depends on how you will use your marketing plan. If you will implement your own marketing plan, incorporate it into your business plan. If you will hire a marketing consultant or an advertising agency to implement your marketing plan, make it a separate document that doesn't require a copy of your business plan to be understood. In some cases, your lender or potential investors will want to see your marketing plan as well as your business plan.

A typical marketing plan will include the following:

- Executive Summary: overview of the plan, short description of your service and how it differs from services offered by other mail order businesses, the required investment and a summary of anticipated sales and profits

- Introduction: a full description of your service and how it fits into the marketplace

- Situation: an analysis of local demand and trends for your service, laws and regulations, financial requirements, competitors and structure of your company including key employees

- Market: describe in more specifics your target market, its size and requirements, its needs and the problems that your mail order product or service will solve for this market

- Strategy: explain how you will reach this target market, the promotional tools you will need, the image you will present and how you will react (or not react) to competitors

- Control: specify how you expect to manage your mail order business to improve your services and increase your share of the customers

---

A marketing plan can be as long or as short as required by its purpose. If you're planning to bring on a big-bucks investor, you will want to develop a detailed marketing plan. However, if you're both the writer and the implementer of the marketing plan, a few pages may be sufficient. In either case, the act of writing will help you clarify your intentions and help you to visualize the outcome. If you want additional guidance on creating a marketing plan to position your mail order business for success, consult *The Market Planning Guide, Fourth Edition* (1995) by David H. Bangs, Jr. (Upstart Publishing).

Selecting Your Business Name

Naming a business is much like naming a baby. In some ways, it will give direction to its growth. A well-named business will seem more successful to prospects and will then become so.

A business name should make it clear to prospects what the firm does or at least the type of products the firm sells. Following are some examples:

- Gifts-by-Mail (denotes the product and how it is delivered to customer)
- Sandra's Gifts (identifies the product, but is personalized at the expense of sounding like a small business)
- Henderson Gifts, Inc. (sounds bigger; surnames are better than first names and "Inc." implies that it is a larger firm— but use it only if your business is incorporated)
- AAA Gifts (specifically identifies the service and assures first-listing in alphabetical directories, such as telephone Yellow Pages)
- Smithtown Services (unclear what service is involved)
- Quality Mail Order Gifts (clearly identifies the product and the owner's attitude)

In selecting a business name, many firms write a defining motto or slogan that is used in all stationery and advertisements to further clarify what the firm does:

- Specializing in unique gifts shipped overnight
- The perfect gift at the perfect time
- Express yourself with the perfect gift
- Thousands of parts in stock
- Offering overnight shipping to the world
- Satisfaction Guaranteed
- Since 1975
- Your One-Stop Source for Gifts

An assumed business name (or dba, for "doing business as") is a name other than the real and true name of each person operating a business. A real and true name becomes an assumed business name with the addition of any words that imply the existence of additional owners. For example, Bob Smith is a real and true name, while Bob Smith Gifts is an assumed business name.

In most states and counties, you must register an assumed business name to let the public know who is transacting business under that name. Without the registration you may be fined or, worse, not be able to defend a legal action because your assumed business name wasn't properly registered.

In many states, an assumed business name is registered with the state's corporate division. Some states will also register your assumed business name with counties in which you do business. Other states require that you do so. In some locations, you must publish a public notice in an area newspaper telling all that you (and any other business principals) are operating under a specific business name.

The typical assumed business name registration requires the following information: the business name you wish to assume, the principal place of business, the name of an authorized representative, your SIC code (standard industrial classification; 5961-02 for a mail order business), a list of all owners with their signatures and a list of all counties in which your firm will transact business (sell, lease, or purchase goods or services; receive funding or credit). Most assumed business name registrations also require a fee.

Locating Your Mail Order Business

Where will you locate your mail order business? The answer depends on your space requirements, your budget and whether you plan to have customers visit your place of business. One distinct advantage to a mail order business is that most customers don't care if you're operating from an office suite or the back of your garage.

Here are some points to consider as you decide where to locate your business:

- Availability of transportation services
- Proximity to source of products
- Physical suitability of building
- Opportunities for future expansion
- Cost of operation
- Tax burden
- Environmental factors
- Personal convenience

The first and most important consideration is making sure that you have easy access to shipping resources. That is, are you located where parcel delivery, postal service and overnight shipping services are readily available? In most locations in the U.S., the answer is yes. However, some locations do not offer as many shipping options as others because fewer transportation services are available. Will you be shipping your products via overnight service? Do they require a trucking service or can a parcel van deliver your products? Considering these factors, let's look at your options.

Home Office

A majority of start-up mail order businesses, especially those that are part-time, operate exclusively from someone's home. Many others start at home and move to business offices as they grow. The entrepreneur sets up a small office at the dining table, in a walk-in closet, in an extra bedroom or in a shop. This is an ideal situation for a part-time mail order business for many reasons. First, there will be little or no additional rent expense. It is also more convenient for you to have all your records at home, where you can review them at any time. In addition, you could ask a family member or someone living with you to answer the telephone while you're away. Finally, you can legally deduct some of your household costs as legitimate expenses and reduce your tax obligation.

But the best reason is that it saves you time. A customer can call you in the evening to ask about a specific job and you can quickly check your records or make notes in the job file without leaving your home. The most popular initial location for a home-based mail order business is a desk in a spare room.

Of course, with a home office you will want to discourage walk-in customers. Don't include your street address in your ads. Rather, have customers send orders to a post office box or mailing service address. In addition, your mail order business may increase truck traffic on your street due to pickups and deliveries. For this reason, you may soon decide to move your growing mail order business to a commercial location.

The IRS says you can deduct part of your home expenses for business purposes. By a home they mean a house, apartment, con-dominium, mobile home, boat, unattached garage, studio, barn or greenhouse. The IRS says that the physical portion of the home you deduct must be used exclusively and regularly in conducting busi-ness. It must be either the principal place of your business, a place where you regularly meet with customers or a separate structure used in connection with your trade. There are more specific definitions of "exclusive use," "regular use" and "principal place of business" in Publication 587.

What home business expenses can you deduct and which can you not? In many cases, you can deduct all expenses directly required by the business no matter where it was located. For example, you can deduct a percentage of your indirect housing expenses, depending on how much of your home is used for the business. Indirect expenses include mortgage interest, real estate taxes, insurance, utilities, depreciation and repairs.

How much you can deduct on the business use of your home

depends on how much of your home is used for business. For example, if your home is 1200 square feet in size and you use 300 square feet or 25 percent of it for your business, you will be able to deduct 25 percent of the indirect expenses of your home.

A word of warning: the home office expense is one of the most abused deductions in the tax system. The IRS more carefully looks at tax filings that include this expense. Most are legitimate, but those who pad their home office expense deductions make it difficult for those who honestly use a portion of their home to conduct business.

Shared Office

You may have friends or relatives who own a related service business such as a retail store or a warehouse. You could share an office or a shop with them, reducing your costs and bringing them some rental income. Of course, don't share an office with anyone who may, in any way, be a competitor or be associated with a competitor. Prospects calling for you could be diverted.

Your Own Office

As your mail order business grows, you will want to move to your own office. The biggest disadvantage of such a move is the cost. But there are many advantages. First, your own office will give you a commercial location for shipping, receiving and warehousing your products and direct mail elements. Second, your business may require that suppliers or lenders come to your office. An office of your own will give them a better first impression. Third, it will give you control over your business that you cannot have if you're working out of a spare bedroom or a shared office.

Many mail order businesses prefer to locate in warehouse complexes with other businesses that use transportation services. Not only is product transportation more convenient, it is frequently less costly per-square-foot of space than prime commercial locations.

Selecting a Site

As mentioned, the most important factor in selecting the site for your mail order business is convenience to transportation services.

Access to a variety of transportation services allows you to use competing delivery systems as needed to keep your costs down. Of course, this is less important if your mail order product or service doesn't require ground or air transportation.

The next most important factor in selecting your business site is the responsiveness of the landlord and the opportunities for negotiating a favorable lease. Make sure your new landlord is continuing to invest in the property, including regular maintenance and quick repairs. And talk with other commercial landlords in your area to ensure that your lease is the best you can negotiate.

You can often get assistance on selecting a commercial site by talking with local and regional chambers of commerce about your needs. They may be able to give you an educated guess on what you will probably have to pay for a property that will help your business become successful.

Zoning Laws

Your mail order location may be limited by local zoning laws. Before deciding where you will set up your business, talk to the local zoning office about restrictions. You may find that so-called cottage or home businesses are allowed in your neighborhood as long as large trucks don't load and unload.

The Americans with Disabilities Act (ADA) requires that business owners offer access to their location that does not restrict employees or customers with disabilities. This act applies to all businesses with 15 or more employees.

Forms of Business

One of the most important decisions you will make as you start your mail order business is what legal form it will take. Why so important? Because how you record expenses, how you build your business, how you pay taxes, how you treat profits and how you manage liability all depend on the structure you give your business.

Of course, as your business grows, you'll be able to move from one type of structure to another, but sometimes there will be a cost. The cost will be paid to the tax man as he decides whether you changed structure to avoid paying your fair share of taxes. One of the reasons you may later change structure is because you want to legally reduce tax liability—and that's okay. It's the abuse of tax laws that brings the wrath of the IRS.

There are four common types of business structures: proprietorship, partnership, corporation and, a relatively new structure, the limited liability company. Each has specific advantages and disadvantages, but they must all be considered against your individual circumstances, goals and needs.

Proprietorship

A sole proprietorship is a business that is owned and operated by one person. However, in many states a business owned jointly by a husband and wife is considered a proprietorship rather than a partnership. This is the easiest form of business to establish. You only need to obtain required licenses and begin operation. For its simplicity, the proprietorship is the most widespread form of small business organization and is especially popular with the new mail order business owner.

The first and most obvious advantage of a proprietorship is ease of formation. There is less formality and fewer legal restrictions associated with establishing a sole proprietorship. It needs little or no governmental approval and is less expensive to start than a partnership or a corporation.

Another advantage of a proprietorship is that it doesn't require that you share profits with anyone. Whatever is left over after you pay the bills (including the tax man) is yours to keep. You will report income, expenses and profit to the IRS, using Schedule C and your standard 1040 form, and make quarterly estimated tax payments to the IRS so you don't get behind before your annual filing.

Control is important to the successful mail order. A proprietorship gives that control and decision-making power to a single person, you. Proprietorships also give the owner flexibility that other forms of business do not. A partner must usually get agreement from other partners. In larger matters, a corporation must get agreement from other members of the board of directors or corporate officers. A proprietor simply makes up his or her mind and acts.

One more plus: the sole proprietor has relative freedom from government control and special taxation. Sure, the government has some say in how you operate and what taxes you will pay. But the government has less to say to the sole proprietor.

Of course, there is a downside to being the only boss, the most important being unlimited liability. That is, the individual proprietor is responsible for the full amount of business debts, which may exceed the proprietor's total investment. With some exceptions, this liability extends to all the proprietor's assets, such as house and car. One way around this is for the proprietor to obtain sufficient insurance coverage to reduce the risk from physical loss and personal injury. But if your suppliers aren't getting paid, they can come after your personal assets.

Another downside is that, when the business is a single individual, the serious illness or death of that person can end the business.

Additionally, individuals typically cannot get the credit and capital that partnerships and corporations can. Fortunately, most mail order businesses don't require extensive capital. But when they do, they seriously consider the advantages of taking on a partner or becoming a corporation.

Finally, as a sole proprietor you have a relatively limited viewpoint and experience because you're only one person. You're more subject to tunnel vision or seeing things in a narrow way based on your experiences. You don't have someone with a commitment to your business who can give you a fresh viewpoint or new ideas.

Partnership

The Uniform Partnership Act (UPA) adopted by many states defines a partnership as "an association of two or more persons to carry on as co-owners of a business for profit." Partnerships are easier and less costly to form than corporations, and, in most states, all that's really needed for their formation is a document called the Articles of Partnership. These describe how the partnership is structured, the powers and limitations of each partner and their participation in the business. The articles or descriptions can either be written by the partners, found in a legal form from a stationery store or written by an attorney. Obviously, using an attorney is the best option because it will ensure that the document is binding and reduce disputes that typically come up once the business is growing.

Your firm's Articles of Partnership should include:

- the name, location, length and purpose of the partnership;

- the type of partnership;

- a definition of the partners' individual contributions;

- an agreement on how business expenses will be handled;

- an outline of the authority of each partner;

- a summary of the accounting methods that will be used;

- a definition of how profits and losses will be distributed among the partners;

- the salaries and capital draws for each partner;

- an agreement of how the partnership will be modified or terminated, including dissolution of the partnership by death or disability of a member or by the decision of partners to disband; and

- a description of how the members will arbitrate and settle disputes as well as change terms of the partnership agreement.

A partnership can typically raise capital more easily than a proprietorship because there are more people whose assets can be combined as equity for the loan. Lenders will look at the credit ratings of each partner, so make sure that your business partners have good credit.

Partnerships are frequently more flexible in the decision-making process than a corporation, but less flexible than a proprietorship.

Like proprietorships, partnerships offer relative freedom from government control and special taxation. A partnership doesn't pay income tax. Rather, all profits and losses flow through the partnership to the individual partners who pay income and other taxes as if they were sole proprietors.

Of course, there are some minuses to partnerships. Like sole proprietorships, at least one partner will be a *general partner* and will assume unlimited liability for the business. The partnership has to obtain sufficient insurance coverage to reduce the financial risk from physical loss or personal injury, but the general partner is still liable.

A partnership is as stable or as unstable as its members. Elimination of any partner often means automatic dissolution of the partnership. However, the business can continue to operate if the agreement includes provisions for the right of survivorship and possible creation of a new partnership. Partnership insurance can assist surviving partners in purchasing the equity of a deceased partner.

Though a partnership has less difficulty in getting financing than a sole proprietorship, the fragile nature of partnerships sometimes makes it difficult to get long-term financing. The best source, as discussed earlier, is using the combined equity of the partners from assets they own as individuals. In fact, many partnerships are started because an active partner needs equity or financing that he cannot get without a partner with more assets or better credit.

Depending upon how the partnership agreement is drawn up, any partner may be able to bind all of the partners to financial obligations. Make sure your Articles of Partnership accurately reflects your intent regarding how partners can or cannot obligate the partnership. Also consider the advantages and disadvantages of structuring your partnership as a limited liability company, discussed in this book right after corporations.

A major drawback to partnerships is the difficulty faced when arranging the departure of a partner. Buying out the partner's interest may be difficult unless terms have been specifically worked out in the partnership agreement.

As you can see, there are numerous pluses and minuses to partnerships. Many of the disadvantages can be addressed in your Articles of Partnership. This is why it is recommended that you use an attorney experienced in such agreements as you construct your partnership. The cost is usually less than the value.

Corporation

Businesses, as they grow, often become corporations, identified by an extension to their name: Corp., Inc., or, in Canada and the United

Kingdom, Ltd. A corporation (called a C corporation) is usually formed by the authority of a state government. The steps to forming a corporation begin with writing incorporation papers and issuing capital stock. Then, approval must be obtained from the secretary of state in the state in which the corporation is being formed. Only then can the corporation act as a legal entity separate from those who own its stock.

The primary advantage to incorporation is that it limits the stockholder's liability to their investment. If you buy $1,000 of stock in a corporation and it fails, you can only lose up to the $1,000 investment. The corporation's creditors cannot come back to you demanding more money. The exception is when you put up some of your own assets as collateral for the corporation.

Ownership of a corporation is a transferable asset. In fact, the New York Stock Exchange and other exchanges make a big business out of transferring stock, or partial ownership, in corporations from one investor to another. If your mail order business is a corporation, you can sell partial ownership or stock in it within certain limits. In fact, this is how many corporations get money to grow. A corporation can also issue long-term bonds to gain cash required to purchase assets or build the business.

Your corporation has a separate and legal existence. Your corporation is not you or anybody else. It is itself. For example, in the case of illness, death or other cause for loss of a corporate officer or owner, the corporation continues to exist and do business.

The corporation can also delegate authority to hired managers, although they are often one and the same. Thus you become an employee of the corporation.

Corporations have disadvantages, too. The corporation's state charter may limit the type of business it does to a specific industry or service. However, other states allow broad charters that permit corporations to operate in any legal enterprise.

Corporations face more governmental regulations on all levels: local, state and federal. That means your business will spend more time and money fulfilling these requirements as a corporation than it would as a proprietorship or a partnership.

If your corporate manager is not also a stockholder, he will have less incentive to be efficient than he would if he had a share in your business.

As you can imagine, a corporation is more expensive to form than other types of businesses. Even if you don't use an attorney, there are forms and fees that will quickly add up. However, an attorney is a good investment when incorporating your mail order business.

Finally, corporations allow the federal and some state governments to tax income twice: once as corporate net income and once as the income is received by the individual stockholders in the form of salary or dividends. A Sub-Chapter S corporation allows small businesses to tax the business as if it were a sole proprietorship or partnership (no corporate income tax) and pass the tax liability on to the individual stockholders. There are about 1.6 million Sub-Chapter S corporations in the U.S. Recent changes in the law may make it easier to get financing for a Sub-S. Talk with an attorney or accountant about this option.

Limited Liability Company

Similar to a partnership, a limited liability company (LLC) is taxed only once on its profits. A C corporation, as mentioned, is taxed twice. Unlike a partnership, an LLC protects partners by limiting their personal liability for actions of the company. An LLC offers liability protections similar to a corporation. In addition, LLCs have fewer restrictions on shareholders and allow the transfer of shares more easily than a corporation. Finally, profits are reported on personal rather than corporate tax returns.

LLCs must be privately held companies. While restructuring a C corporation into an LLC can be difficult and costly, changing your business from an LLC to a C corporation is quite easy. One major drawback to LLCs is that their limitation of liability has not been extensively tested in the court system, as has the liability of corporations. If you select to establish an LLC, make sure you have an attorney who has experience with this structure and who can advise you based on liability and tax issues in your state.

About 40 states recognize limited liability companies as a legal business structure. They have been popular in other countries for many years. In establishing an LLC, you will need to file articles of organization and an operating agreement with state authorities. For more information on LLCs, contact the Association of Limited Liability Companies (202-965-6565). *A Guide to Limited Liability*

Companies is available from Commerce Clearing House (800-835-5224).

Selecting an Attorney

To find an attorney who is familiar with a business of your size and trade, ask for a referral from a business colleague, your banker, your accountant, your local chamber of commerce or other business services in your area. Many local bar associations run an attorney referral and information service; check your local telephone book's Yellow Pages under "Attorneys' Referral & Information Services." Some referral services give you only names and phone numbers; others actually give information on experience and fees to help you match your needs to the attorney's background and charges. If possible, you want an attorney with experience serving the legal needs of mail order businesses. At the least, the attorney should have experience with small businesses.

An attorney can help you decide which is the most advantageous business structure for you. He or she can also help you with zoning, licensing problems, unpaid bills, contracts and agreements, employment laws, copyright questions, trademarks and some tax problems.

Because there is always the possibility of a lawsuit, claim or other legal action against your business, it is wise to have an attorney who is already familiar with your business lined up before a crisis arises. An attorney with experience serving employment service businesses can also advise you on federal, state and local laws, and on programs and agencies to help you prepare for or prevent potential problems.

Let your attorney know that you expect to be informed of all developments and consulted before any decisions are made on your behalf. You may also want to receive copies of all documents, letters and memos written and received regarding your project. If this isn't practical, you should at least have the opportunity to read such correspondence at your attorney's office.

Another valuable legal resource is the *Mail Order Legal Guide* (Oasis Press, 800-228-2275). It includes extensive information on the legal aspects of direct mail sales.

If you must copyright your mail order product, first contact the Register of Copyrights, Copyright Office, Washington, DC 20559-6000 (202-707-9100) for forms and requirements.

Selecting an Accountant

Many new mail order businesses fail because of poor financial management. Sometimes the best decision a new business owner makes is to hire the services of a public accounting firm. An accountant can design recordkeeping systems, set up ways for maintaining records, analyze financial information and help you relate that information to profitability.

Daily bits of information will flow into your mail order business. As you serve customers, you will generate information about sales, cash, supplies, purchase expenses, payroll, accounts payable and, if credit is offered to customers, accounts receivable.

To capture these facts and figures, a system is necessary. If you don't feel comfortable with setting up and managing such a system, don't be shy about hiring an accounting service. An accountant can help design one for recording the information that you need to control finances and make profitable decisions.

Once a system of records has been set up, the question is: Who should keep the books? The accounting service who has set up the books may keep them. However, if you have a general understanding of recordkeeping you can do them yourself and save some money. Use your accountant for checking and analyzing your records. Once your business has grown, you may want to hire someone to keep your records and perform other office functions.

In addition to recordkeeping, an accountant can advise you on financial management, providing you with cash flow requirements, budget forecasts, borrowing, business organization and tax information.

By analyzing cash flow requirements, an accountant can help you work out the amount of cash needed to operate your firm during a specific period—for example, three months, six months, the next year. He or she considers how much cash you will need to carry customer accounts receivable, to buy equipment and supplies, to pay current bills and to repay loans. In addition, an accountant can determine how much cash will come from collection of accounts receivable and how much will have to be borrowed or pulled from an existing line of credit. While working out the cash requirements, your accountant may notice and call your attention to danger spots such as accounts that are past due.

If you're applying for a loan, your accountant can assemble financial information, for example, a profit-and-loss or income statement and a balance sheet. The purpose of such data is to show the lender the financial position of your business and its ability to repay the loan. Using this information, your accountant can advise you on whether you need a short-term or long-term loan. If you have never borrowed before, your accountant may help you by introducing you to a lender who knows and respects the accountant's reputation. This, alone, may be worth the cost of hiring an accountant.

Taxes are another area in which an accountant can contribute advice and assistance. Normally, a recordkeeping system that provides the information you need for making profitable decisions will suffice for tax purposes. However, if you purchase equipment that requires special depreciation, have employees who handle cash or require payroll taxes, or have extensive bad debts, a good accountant can help you identify the problems, suggest a method of keeping good records and help you minimize your tax obligation by writing off bad debts as a business expense. Accounting firms will also get your federal and state withholding numbers for you, instruct you on where and when to file tax returns, prepare tax returns and do general tax planning for your small business.

In looking for an accountant, get referrals from trusted friends, business associations, professional associations and other business services. Discuss fees in advance and draw up a written agreement about how you will work together. Your accountant is your key financial adviser. He or she should alert you to potential danger areas and advise you on how to handle growth spurts, how to best plan for slow business times and how to financially mature and protect your business future from unnecessary risk.

Selecting an Insurance Agent

The agent is the insurance industry's primary client representative, and a good agent is as valuable to your success as any other professional consultant. An experienced and trustworthy insurance agent can both reduce your exposure to risk and keep your insurance costs to a minimum. Typically, the independent agent is a small business owner and manager. By using this distribution system, insurance companies are represented by agents who receive a commission for selling the companies' products and services. An independent agent may represent more than one insurance company.

Ask around among other business services and professionals for recommendations of a good insurance agent. If possible, search for one who primarily serves the business community rather than the family or individuals. They will better know your problems and concerns.

Ask prospective agents for some advice on a specific problem. Don't tell them what you think the solution is. Their responses can help you determine who are the best at cost-effective problem solving.

Liability insurance coverages, particularly for property damage and bodily injury, usually include legal defense at no additional charge when the policyholder is named a party to the lawsuit that involves a claim covered by the policy. Litigation is costly, whether the claimant's suit is valid or frivolous. The legal defense provision greatly reduces these costs to you.

Action Guidelines

Starting up your mail order business requires a number of important steps: testing your business idea, estimating start-up costs, selecting your business name, locating your business, choosing the form of your business and selecting your professional advisers. Here's how to implement what you've learned in Chapter 4.

Start writing your business plan. Refer to *The Business Planning Guide*, by David H. Bangs, Jr., and other resources for worksheets and examples.

✔ Write your business's statement of purpose.

✔ Select your business name and find out how to register and protect it.

✔ Develop a slogan or motto that best fits your business.

✔ Decide where to initially locate your business. Research and consider many sites, writing information in your mail order notebook.

✔ Decide which form of business you will initially use: proprietorship, partnership, corporation or limited liability company.

✔ Find a good attorney.

✔ Find a good accountant.

✔ Find a good insurance agent.

OPERATING YOUR
MAIL ORDER BUSINESS

Starting a business is only part of your goal. To succeed you must manage its daily operation. You must control operating costs, keep and analyze records, price and provide products by mail, hire and manage employees, and pay taxes.

This chapter covers these and other responsibilities of your mail order business's daily operations as suggested by successful business men and women. It will help you understand and focus on the nuts and bolts of your business as you keep your eyes on the broader purpose of your venture: to help others as you help yourself.

Estimating Your Operating Costs

Managing your mail order business requires that you manage your business budget so you can continue to provide service and support to others as well as a profit to yourself. When you first started your business, you established a preliminary budget. Now that your business is operating, you must establish an operating budget.

A budget is a forecast of all cash sources and cash expenditures. It is organized in the same format as a financial statement and most commonly covers a 12-month period. At the end of the year, the projected income and expenses in the budget are compared to the actual performance as recorded in the financial statement.

A budget can greatly enhance your chances of success by helping you estimate future needs and plan profits, spending and overall cash flow. A budget allows you to detect problems before they occur and to alter your plans to prevent those problems.

In business, budgets help you determine how much money you have and how you will use it, as well as help you decide whether you have enough money to achieve your financial goals. As part of your business plan, a budget can help convince a loan officer that you know your business and have anticipated its needs.

A budget will indicate the cash required for necessary labor and materials, the day-to-day operating costs, the revenue needed to support business operations and expected profit. If your budget indicates that you need more revenue than you can earn, you can adjust your plans by:

- reducing expenditures (hiring independent contractors or part-time, rather than full-time, employees, purchasing less expensive furniture, eliminating an extra telephone line);
- expanding sales (offering additional products, conducting an aggressive marketing campaign, researching new markets); and
- lowering your salary or profit expectations.

There are three main elements to a budget: sales revenue, total costs and profit.

Sales are the cornerstone of a budget. It is crucial to estimate anticipated sales as accurately as possible. If available, base estimates on actual past sales figures or use conservative sales estimates. Once you target sales, you can calculate the related expenses necessary to achieve your goals.

Total costs include fixed and variable costs. Estimating costs is complicated because you must identify which costs will change—and by how much—and which costs will remain unchanged as sales increase. You must also consider inflation and rising prices when appropriate.

Variable costs are those that vary directly with sales. Shipping expenses are examples of variable costs for your mail order business. Fixed costs are those that don't change regardless of sales volume, such as rent or salaries. Semivariable costs, such as telephone expenses, have both variable and fixed components. Part of the expense is listed as fixed (telephone line charges) and part is variable (long-distance charges).

Profit should be large enough to make a return on cash investment and your labor. Your investment is the money you put into the firm at start-up and the profit from prior years that you have left in the firm (retained earnings). If you can receive 10 percent interest on $10,000 by investing outside of your business, then you should expect a similar return when investing $10,000 in equipment and other assets within the business. In targeting profits, you also want to be sure you're receiving a fair return on your labor. Your weekly paycheck should reflect what you could be earning elsewhere as an employee.

Establishing an Operating Budget

As you develop your budget, you'll be working with the budget equation. The basic budget equation is:

$$Sales = Total\ Costs + Profit$$

This equation shows that every sales dollar you receive is made up partly of a recovery of your costs and partly of profit. Another way to express the basic budgeting equation is:

$$Sales - Total\ Costs = Profit$$

This equation shows that, after reimbursing yourself for the cost of producing your service, the remaining part of the sales dollar is gross profit. For example, if you expect $1,000 for a specific direct mail campaign and you know that it will cost $900 to market and fulfill, your gross profit will be $100.

In calculating an operating budget, you will often make estimates based on past sales and cost figures. You will need to adjust these figures to reflect price increases, inflation and other factors. For example, during the past three years, a mail order business owner spent an average of $5,000 on advertising costs per year. For the coming year, the owner expects an advertising cost increase of 5 percent (0.05). To calculate next year's advertising costs, the owner multiplies the average annual advertising costs by the percentage price increase ($5,000 × 0.05 = $250) and adds that amount to the original annual cost ($5,000 + $250 = $5,250). A shortcut method is to multiply the original advertising cost by one plus the rate of increase ($5,000 × 1.05 = $5,250).

If your mail order business is a new venture and has no past financial records, rely on your own experience and knowledge of the industry to estimate demand for and costs of your service. Your accountant or trade association may also be able to help you develop realistic estimates.

Before you create an operating budget, you must answer three questions:

1. How much net profit do you realistically want your business to generate during the calendar year?
2. How much will it cost to produce that profit?
3. How much sales revenue is necessary to support both profit and cost requirements?

To answer these questions, consider expected sales and all costs, either direct or indirect, associated with your mail order business. To make the safest estimates when budgeting, most companies prefer to overestimate expenses and underestimate sales revenue.

Start constructing your budget with either a forecast of sales or a forecast of profits. For practical purposes, most small businesses start with a forecast of profits. In other words, decide what profit you realistically want to make and then list the expenses you will incur to make that profit.

How To Keep Good Records

Why keep records? There are many reasons. For the individual just starting a mail order business, an adequate recordkeeping system increases the chances of survival. Also, an established mail order business can enhance its chances of staying in business and increasing profits with a good recordkeeping system.

Following are some of the questions that good business records can answer:

- How much business am I doing?
- How much credit am I extending?
- How are my collections?
- What are my losses from credit sales?
- Who owes me money?
- Who is delinquent?
- Should I continue extending credit to delinquent accounts?
- How much cash do I have on hand?
- How much cash do I have in the bank?
- Does this amount agree with what records tell me I should have or is there a shortage?
- How much have I invested in supplies?
- How often do I turn over my supplies inventory?
- How much do I owe my suppliers and other creditors?
- How much gross profit or margin did I earn?
- What were my expenses?
- What's my weekly payroll?
- Do I have adequate payroll records to meet the requirements of workers' compensation insurance, wage-and-hour laws, Social Security insurance, unemployment compensation insurance and withholding taxes?
- How much net profit did I earn?
- How much income taxes will I owe?
- Are my sales, expenses, profits and capital showing improvements or did I do better last year than this?

- How do I stand as compared with two periods ago?

- Is my business's position about the same, improving or deteriorating?

- On what services am I making a profit, breaking even or losing money?

- Am I taking full advantage of cash discounts for prompt payments?

- Are the discounts I get from suppliers as great as those I give to my customers?

- How do the financial facts of my mail order business compare with those of similar businesses?

Get the point? Your business requires a good recordkeeping system to help you work smarter rather than harder.

Keeping accurate and up-to-date business records is, for many people, the most difficult and dull aspect of operating a business. If this area of business management is one that you believe will be hard for you, plan now how you will handle this task. Don't wait until tax time or until you're totally confused. Take a course at a local community college, ask a volunteer SCORE representative or hire an accountant to advise you on setting up and maintaining your record-keeping system.

Your records will be used to prepare tax returns, make business decisions and apply for loans. Set aside a special time each day to update your records. It will pay off in the long run with more deductions and fewer headaches.

A good recordkeeping system should be:

- simple to use,

- easy to understand,

- reliable,

- accurate,

- consistent, and

- timely.

Several published systems and software systems provide simplified records, usually in a single record book. These systems cover the primary records required for all businesses, but some are modified specifically for the mail order business. Check your local office supply store, your trade association or trade journals for more information on specialized record books.

Simply, your records should tell you these three facts:

1. How much cash you owe
2. How much cash is owed to you
3. How much cash you have on hand

To keep track of everything, you should have these basic journals:

- A sales journal (Figure 5.1, on page 84) shows the business transaction, when and for whom it was performed, and the amount of the invoice.
- A cash receipts journal (Figure 5.2, on page 85) shows the amount of money received, from whom and for what.
- A cash disbursements journal (Figure 5.3, on page 86), or check register, shows each check disbursed, the date of the disbursement, number of the check, to whom it was made out (payee), the amount of money disbursed and for what purpose.
- A general journal for noncash transactions and those involving the owner's equity in the business.

In addition, following are other records you will need in your business:

- Aging accounts receivable (Figure 5.4, on page 87) is the record of accounts on which you are due money from a sale for which you haven't been fully paid.
- Aging accounts payable is the record of accounts for which you will have to pay money because you have purchased a product or service but haven't paid for it all.
- Inventory record (Figure 5.5, on page 88) lists your firm's investment in paper, envelopes, books, videos and other items you intend to resell.

Gifts By Mail

Great Gifts for Great Friends

**123 Main St.
Yourtown USA
800-555-GIFT**

Sales Journal

PERIOD ENDING:

Date	Invoice Number	Account Number	Name	Amount

Figure 5.1: Sales journal.

Gifts By Mail

Great Gifts for Great Friends

123 Main St.
Yourtown USA
800-555-GIFT

Cash Receipts Journal

PERIOD ENDING:

Date	Check Number	Account Number	Name	Amount

Figure 5.2: Cash receipts journal.

Gifts By Mail

Great Gifts for Great Friends

**123 Main St.
Yourtown USA
800-555-GIFT**

Cash Disbursements Journal

PERIOD ENDING:

Date	Check Number	Account Number	Name	Amount

Figure 5.3: Cash disbursements journal.

Gifts By Mail

Great Gifts for Great Friends

**123 Main St.
Yourtown USA
800-555-GIFT**

Aging Accounts Receivable

PERIOD ENDING:

INVOICE DATE	INVOICE #	ACCOUNT #	ACCOUNT NAME	30 DAYS	60 DAYS	90+DAYS	TOTAL
				TOTALS			
				GRAND TOTAL DUE			

Figure 5.4: Aging accounts receivable.

Gifts By Mail

Great Gifts for Great Friends

123 Main St.
Yourtown USA
800-555-GIFT

Inventory Record

Department :		Location:		Date	Page	of

Item#	Quantity	Description	Price	Total
			TOTAL	

Priced By:	Called By:
Checked By:	Entered By:

Figure 5.5: Inventory record.

- Equipment record is a list of your firm's investment in equipment that you will use in providing your service and will not normally resell.

- Payroll is a record of the wages of employees and their deductions for income, FICA and other taxes as well as other payroll deductions. Figure 5.6 (on page 90) is a typical daily time report from which payroll information is gathered.

Some businesses combine all of these journals into a single journal. In fact, there are many good one-write systems available that allow you to make a single entry for each transaction. You can also use computer software such as Quicken, QuickBooks, Manage Your Money or Microsoft Money to track income and expenses in a checkbook format. More extensive accounting software programs include DacEasy Accounting, M.Y.O.B., Pacioli 2000 and Peachtree. All are available through leading software retailers and mail order catalogs.

Recordkeeping Systems

There are two ways to record transactions in your business: with a single entry or with a double entry. The primary advantage to single-entry recordkeeping is that it is easy. As the name implies, you make a single entry that records the source of each income or destination of each expense. Each entry is either a plus or a minus to the amount of cash that you have. Receipt of a check on an outstanding account is a plus. Payment of a supplies order is a minus. As long as you have a limited number of transactions, single-entry accounting is adequate.

However, as your mail order business grows in complexity, you will want a check-and-balance system that ensures that records are accurate. Double-entry accounting requires that you make two off-setting entries that balance each other. A check received on an outstanding account is a debit to cash and a credit to accounts receivable. Payment for a supplies order is a debit to supplies and a credit to cash.

Every account has two sides: a left or debit side and a right or credit side. The posted debits must always equal the posted credits. Some types of accounts are called debit accounts because their balance

Gifts By Mail

Great Gifts for Great Friends

123 Main St.
Yourtown USA
800-555-GIFT

Daily Time Sheet

LOCATION / ORG. UNIT:			DATE:
NAMES	**HOURS**	**CLASSIFICATION**	**DESCRIPTION OF WORK**

REMARKS:

The undersigned employee certifies that the above and foregoing is the actual, correct number of hours worked by him/her on the day stated, and that he/she has not been told or instructed by anyone having authority over him/her to incorrectly state the number of hours actually worked.

Employee's Signature _____

Supervisor's Signature _____

Figure 5.6: Daily time sheet.

is typically a debit. Asset accounts (cash, accounts receivable) are debit accounts. Liability accounts (accounts payable, notes payable) usually carry a credit balance. Income carries a credit balance while expenses carry a debit balance.

Following are some examples of common double entries:

- Cash income = debit cash and credit income
- Credit or accrued income = debit accounts receivable and credit income
- Cash expense = debit the expense account and credit cash
- Credit or accrued expense = debit the expense account and credit accounts payable
- Prepaid expense = debit prepaid expenses and credit cash

If, at the end of the month, the debits don't equal the credits, check for debits erroneously posted as credits, credits erroneously posted as debits, transposition of numbers (123 to 132) and incorrect math.

Assets, Liabilities and Net Worth

Assets include not only cash, inventory, land, building, equipment, furniture and the like, but also money due from individuals or other businesses (known as accounts or notes receivable).

Liabilities are funds acquired for a business through loans or the sale of property or services to the business on credit. Creditors do not acquire ownership in your business, but promissory notes to be paid at a designated future date (known as accounts or notes payable).

Net worth (or shareholders' equity or capital) is money put into a business by its owners or left in it as retained earnings for use by the business in acquiring assets.

The formula for this structure is:

Assets = Liabilities + Net Worth

That is, the total funds invested in assets of the business are equal to the funds supplied to the business by its creditors plus the funds supplied to the business by its owners. If a business owes more money to creditors than it possesses in value of assets owned and retained earnings, the net worth or owner's equity of the business will be a negative number.

This accounting formula can also be expressed as:

$$\text{Assets} - \text{Liabilities} = \text{Net Worth}$$

Cash or Accrual?

Many small businesses are operated primarily on a *cash basis*. The customer buys products with cash or credit card and the merchant buys inventory with cash or short-term credit. As businesses become larger and more complicated, many keep records on the accrual basis. The dividing line between cash basis and accrual basis might depend on whether or not credit is given to customers as well as the amount of inventory required.

Accrual basis is a method of recording income and expenses in which each item is reported as earned or incurred, without regard as to when actual payments are received or made. Income and related expenses are recorded in the same year. Charge sales are credited at once to sales and charged to accounts receivable. When the bills are collected, the credit is to accounts receivable.

Accruals should also be made for larger expense items payable in the future, such as annual or semi-annual interest on loans.

If you're comfortable with accounting, accrual can be the most accurate basis for records. But the cash basis is easiest to understand. As long as you don't prepay many of your expenses and are not incorporated, a cash basis is fine for your new mail order business.

Managing Accounts Receivable

Income not paid to you is called *accounts receivable*. Following are a few rules that can help you keep accounts receivable current. First, be sure bills are prepared immediately after the service is performed and the statement is mailed to the correct person and address and contains sufficient information to fully identify the source and purpose of the charge. Note that some businesses will simply set aside any bills that they question.

At the end of each month, age your accounts receivable if your mail order business has any. That is, list accounts and enter the amounts that are current, those unpaid for 30 days and those more than 60 days old. In fact, most accounts receivable computer programs will produce reports on aged receivables; then call each account in the 60-plus days column and find out why the bill is unpaid. Keep an especially close watch on larger accounts.

To ensure that you get paid promptly, pay close attention to customers' complaints about bills. If a complaint is justified, offer an adjustment and reach an agreement with the customer. Then get a date from the customer as to when you can expect to receive the payment.

Managing Payroll Records

If you hire employees for your mail order business, quarterly and yearly reports of individual payroll payments must be made to federal and, in many cases, state governments. Each individual employee must receive a W-2 form by January 31 showing total withholding payments made for the employee during the previous year.

A payroll summary should be made each payday showing the names, employee numbers, rates of pay, hours worked, overtime hours, total pay, and amount of deductions for FICA (Social Security insurance), Medicare insurance, state and federal withholding taxes, deductions for insurance, pension, savings and child support, as required.

To ensure that you maintain adequate records for this task, keep an employee card for each employee of your firm. The employee card or computer file should show the full legal name, Social Security insurance number, address, telephone number, name of next of kin and their address, marital status, number of exemptions claimed, and current rate of pay. A federal W-4 form completed and signed by the employee should also be attached to the employee card or record.

Also maintain a running total of earnings, pay and deductions for each individual employee.

In addition, if your business employs union members, you may have additional deductions for union dues, pensions, and other fees.

To begin your payroll system, contact the Internal Revenue Service (Washington, DC 20224) and request the Employer's Tax Guide (Circular E) and get a nine-digit Employer Identification Number. The IRS will then send you deposit slips (Form 8109) with your new ID number printed on them. Use these deposit slips each time you pay your payroll taxes. Payroll taxes are paid within a month of the ending of a quarter; that is, January 31, April 30, July 31 and October 31. As your business grows, you may be required to pay payroll taxes more frequently. By then, your accountant will help you determine your needs and the process.

Managing Petty Cash

Most business expenses will be paid by business check, credit card or placed on account with the seller. However, there may be some small expenses that will be paid by an employee or with cash that require reimbursement. Because the amount is typically small, the fund from which the reimbursement comes is usually known as *petty cash.*

A petty cash fund should be set up to be used for payments of small amounts not covered by invoices. A check should be drawn for, say, $100. The check is cashed and the fund placed in a box or drawer. When small cash payments are made for such items as postage, shipping or supplies, the items are listed on a printed form or even a slip of paper. When the fund is nearly exhausted, the items are summarized and a check drawn to cover the exact amount spent. The check is cashed and the fund replenished. At all times, the cash in the drawer plus the listed expenditures should equal the established amount of the petty cash fund.

Equipment Records

Keep an accurate and up-to-date list of permanent equipment used in your mail order business. Especially, keep track of equipment useful for a year or longer and of appreciable value. Equipment records should show date purchased, name of seller, description of item, check number of payment(s), and amount of purchase including tax. If you own a number of items, keep a separate list for vehicles, computers and printers, mailing equipment and office furniture. From these records you will develop a depreciation worksheet and provide supporting information for fixed asset accounts.

Depreciation is a deduction from your taxes for a portion of the expense of a long-term asset used in your business. For example, the cost of a truck purchased for use by your business can be depreciated or spread out over more than one tax year. A business truck is typically a five-year property, meaning that its cost can be spread out over five years.

A recordkeeping entry to expenses should be made to cover depreciation of fixed assets other than land. Fixed assets are any items you purchase to use in your business for a year or longer. Examples are buildings, vehicles, equipment, furniture and office fixtures. Smaller businesses will usually charge depreciation at the end of their fiscal year, but if your business grows and you have major fixed assets, you or your accountant may decide to calculate depreciation monthly.

As clarification, a calendar year is 12 consecutive months beginning January 1 and ending December 31. A fiscal year is 12 consecutive months ending on the last day of any month other than December. A short tax year is less than 12 months because your firm was not in business a full year or you have changed your tax year.

How To Price Your Mail Order Products

You might consider that this question—how much should I charge?—is one of the most important questions of the book. It really isn't. Many other questions will be just as important to the success of your business. However, this question is often the first one that new mail order businesses ask. So let's get it answered, first by considering the three Cs of pricing:

- Cost
- Competition
- Customer

Ask yourself, How much does my mail order product cost me to furnish? Once you've established your start-up costs and your monthly operating costs, you'll have a good idea of how much your products will cost you to furnish to your customers.

How do you know if your pricing is profitable for you? Direct mail is a cost-effective way to reach customers, and the outcome can be predicted. A mail order offer can be measured for success by subtracting direct mail expenses from the selling price of the product.

How much are my competitors charging? By becoming a customer of your competitors you will be able to track their prices. Of course, you must make sure that you're comparing apples with apples. Your competitor may not be selling the same quality of products or services that you are. Or your competitor may be including production or fulfillment costs that you don't have.

Why should you care what your competitors charge? Because your customers will probably get direct mail materials from them also. You don't necessarily have to match or beat their prices, but you do need to know what their rates are so that you can help the customer make a fair comparison.

How much do the customers expect to pay? Remember that the question isn't how much will customers pay, it's how much do they expect to pay? The difference is expectation. You may get some customers to pay a higher price for a while, but they'll soon move to other sources. What you want to find out is what they think your service is actually worth to them. Most understand that, if they pay you too little, you will soon be out of business and won't be there able to help them in the future. They may not admit to it, but they know it.

How can you know how much the consumer expects to pay for your products? Ask a few of them. They may tell you what they're used to paying, what they think is a fair price, or maybe what they wish they were paying. Take them all into consideration. Ask the question of them and let them take a few minutes to explain why they think so. You'll get some valuable insight into what customers expect from you as well as what you should expect from them.

How can you develop a price list that is both profitable and competitive? By knowing what it costs to furnish your product as well as how much your competitors charge for a similar product.

For example, you may determine that your primary product, a correspondence course in paralegal careers, should sell for $295. You know that your competitors are charging $195 for the same product. What should you do?

If you want to undercut your competitor (and maybe start a price war), you can price the package at $175 and still make a profit. Or you can offer it at the same price as your competitor and offer something your competition doesn't offer, such as job placement services or additional reference materials. Or you can compete by comparing the features and value of your course over that of your competitors. Customers want value. So let's talk more about value.

Selling Value

Now you know what your time costs you, what your competitors charge for their products as well as what customers expect to pay for your products. So which figure is right? All and none. What you want is a price that will drive away about 10 percent of your prospects as too high and another 10 percent as too low.

Here's a technique that will make your business more profitable, put your business above your competitors and keep your customers happy: sell value not price. How can a fancy restaurant charge five times as much as the diner next door for the exact same ingredients? They sell value. Call it ambiance or image or snobbery or nonprice considerations or whatever. The fancy restaurant makes the customer's purchase an event rather than just a transaction. The fancy restaurant treats the customer like a person rather than a number, gives extra service, uses finer dinnerware and decorates the food to look appetizing.

You'll see the same technique—selling value rather than price—in any competitive business where one firm wants to stand out above the others. Chevys are sold on price; Cadillacs are sold on value—and both are built by General Motors. Value says that, whether the price is large or small, you will get your money's worth.

So how does a mail order business owner sell value? By offering products that other mail order businesses do not, by paying all shipping charges or by simply turning questions of price into discussions of value.

There are many valuable extra services that a mail order business owner can perform for customers that don't cost much to implement yet add value to the service. Depending on the type of work done, some mail order businesses offer free shipping on all orders or on orders over a specific amount. The cost to the mail order business is minimal and is usually factored into the price, but the extra value is something that your competitors may not offer.

Imagine seeing on the grocer's shelf a can of tomato sauce that was discolored and dented, the label torn. You'd probably pass it by for one that looked neat, fresh and undamaged. Yet the contents of each can may be exactly the same quality. Appearance does make a difference—especially in the mail order business. For just a few dollars more, your business can develop a clean, professional appearance that will tell prospects and customers that you offer quality. Make sure your direct mail packages and even your shipping packages reflect the image that you want to present to your customers.

Price is the cost of something. Value is the worth of something. Why is your product worth something? Successful mail order businesses don't shun the question of pricing or apologize for higher prices. They look forward to the question so that they can explain why their products are worth more than that of other mail order offers. They sell—and deliver—value.

Your Workday

By breaking down your mail order business into specific tasks and scheduling each one, you can help ensure that all tasks are completed on time.

You can also prioritize your jobs into most important, less important and least important to make sure that you're always doing what's most valuable to your business. A most important job is one with the shortest deadline, the quickest payout, the most important task, the greatest opportunity for your mail order business firm. That means, give highest priority to tasks that provide your business with the greatest cash flow (cash, net 15 days, etc.) before those that don't directly increase sales (reading mail order trade journals).

Of course, this doesn't mean that any of your tasks are really less important than any other. All have equal potential for helping your business succeed, and some, if left unattended to, can cause your business to fail. But the task that directly increases your mail order sales today is of greater value than one that can be completed anytime in the next month. So you prioritize your work based your business's needs as well as your own.

Besides prioritizing, group similar jobs together during the same time period, if possible, such as prepackaging many orders at once to reduce fulfillment time.

A monthly planner can help with long-term planning and help you develop your daily planner or list of things to do.

How To Hire Good Employees

The best way to hire the right person for the job is to clearly define what skills are needed. Once you know what it takes to do the job, you can match the applicant's skills and experience to the job's requirements. This step will probably be easy for you if you're hiring someone to take over part of your primary tasks, but how about office help or other support functions?

Once you have a job description on paper, decide what skills the person must have to fill the job. Then, estimate the value of this service to your business. Finally, determine how much other employers in your area are paying for these skills.

When you know the kinds of skills you need in your new employee and their market value, you're ready to contact sources that can help you recruit job applicants.

Each state has an employment service (Department of Employment, Unemployment Bureau or Employment Security Agency). All are affiliated with the United States Employment Service, and local offices are ready to help businesses with their hiring problems. The state employment service will screen applicants for you by giving aptitude tests (if any are available for the skills you need). Passing scores indicate the applicant's ability to learn the work. Be as specific as you can about the skills you want.

Private employment agencies will also help in recruitment. However, the employee or the employer must pay a fee to the private agency for its services. This fee can be the equivalent of from a month's to as much as a year's salary of the employee hired through the agency.

Another source of applicants is a "Help Wanted" sign in your own office window (if you have one). Of course, a lot of unqualified applicants may inquire about the job, and you cannot simultaneously interview an applicant and talk on the phone to a customer.

Newspaper advertisements are another source of applicants. You reach a large group of job seekers, and if you use a blind box address, you can screen them at your convenience. If you list an office phone number, you may end up on the phone with an applicant instead of with a customer.

Job applicants are readily available from local schools. The local high school may have a distributive or cooperative education department where the students work in your office part time while taking trade or business courses at school. Many part-time students continue with their employer after they finish school. Consider local and regional business schools as well. The students are often more mature and more motivated than high school students.

You may also find job applicants by contacting friends, neighbors, customers, suppliers, current employees, local associations, service clubs or even a nearby armed forces base where people are leaving the service. However, don't overlook the problems of such recruiting. What happens to the goodwill of these sources if they recommend a friend whom you do not hire or if you have to fire the person they recommend?

Your choice of recruitment method depends on what you're looking for, your location and your method of managing your business. You have many sources available to you. A combination may serve your best needs. The important thing is to find the right applicant with the correct skills for the job you want to fill, whatever the source.

A good employee is one who is skilled, reliable and trustworthy. You may be the best judge of the applicant's skills, but how do you test reliability? Fortunately, there are standardized tests you can administer to measure potential of substance abuse, courtesy, maturity, conscientiousness, trustworthiness, commitment and attitudes toward safety. One such test is produced by Wonderlic Personnel Tests, Inc. (1509 N. Milwaukee Ave., Libertyville, IL 60048; 800-323-3742) and requires about 15 minutes to complete the 81 true/false statements. The test is available in paper and computerized versions. The test costs less than $12 each. Wonderlic also offers a personnel test that measures the applicant's ability to understand instructions, potential for learning a job quickly, ability to solve job related problems and ability to work creatively. Such tests can help you profitably find and manage better employees.

Employment Laws You Must Know About

As you begin searching for employees, there are certain laws, federal and state, that come into play. Your local state employment office can assist you in learning the current requirements of these laws.

The Social Security Act of 1935, as amended, is concerned with employment insurance laws as well as retirement insurance.

The Fair Labor Standards Act of 1938, as amended, establishes minimum wages, overtime pay, recordkeeping and child labor standards for most businesses.

The Occupational Safety and Health Act (OSHA) of 1970 is concerned with safety and health in the workplace and covers almost all employers. There are specific standards, regulations and reporting requirements that must be met.

There are other laws that may concern your business. Contact your local state employment office to determine the requirements for hiring disadvantaged workers, federal service contracts for work on public buildings or other public projects, employee pension and welfare benefit plans, and the garnishment of an employee's wages.

In addition, the Immigration Reform and Control Act of 1986 prohibits employing illegal aliens. You must require every employee to fill out the Employment Eligibility Verification Form (Form 19) within three days of the date of hire (if hired after November 7, 1987). Fines are levied for noncompliance. For more information, contact the nearest office of the Immigration and Naturalization Service.

The Civil Rights Act of 1964 prohibits discrimination in employment practices because of race, religion, sex or national origin. Public Law 90-202 prohibits discrimination on the basis of age with respect to individuals who are between 40 and 70 years of age. Federal laws also prohibit discrimination against the physically handicapped. Again, your state employment office can help you in understanding the laws regarding applicants and employment. In addition, firms like G. Neil (720 International Parkway, Sunrise, FL

33345) offer catalogs of human relations supplies: job applications, personnel folders, labor law posters, attendance controllers, employee awards and related materials.

The Application Form

The hardest part of the hiring process, once you've listed the required skills, is in finding and hiring the one right employee. You need some method of screening the applicants and selecting the best one for the position.

A preprinted employment application form is a tool that you can use to make your tasks of interviewing and selection easier. The form should have blank spaces for all the facts you need as a basis for judging the applicants.

You will want a fairly complete application so you can get sufficient information. However, keep the form as simple as you can. Have the applicants fill out the application before you interview them as it makes an excellent starting point. It is also a written record of experience and former employers' names and addresses.

When an applicant has had work experience, other references are typically not as important. However, if the level of work experience is limited, additional references may be obtained from other individuals such as school counselors who may be able to offer objective information.

Personal references are almost useless as an applicant would only list people who have a kind word for them. Some employers will use them, rather, to open a discussion, asking such questions as:

- What would this reference say were your greatest skills and traits?
- What would this reference say were skills and traits that you needed to work on?

Interviewing Job Applicants

The objective of the job interview is to find out as much information as you can about the job applicant's work background, especially work habits and skills. Your major task is to get the applicants to talk about themselves and about their work habits. The best way to go about this is to ask each applicant specific questions:

- What did you do on your last job?
- How did you do it?
- Why was it done?
- What were the results?

As you go along, evaluate the applicants' replies. Do they know what they are talking about? Are they evasive or unskilled in the job tasks? Can they account for discrepancies in their employment record?

When the interview is over, ask the applicant to check back with you later, if you think you may be interested in that applicant. Never commit yourself until you have interviewed all likely applicants. You want to be sure that you select the best available applicant for the job.

Next, verify the information you've obtained. A previous employer is usually the best source. Sometimes a previous employer will give out information over the phone. But, if you have the time, it is usually best to request your information in writing and get a written reply.

To help insure a prompt reply from the applicant's previous employers, you should ask a few specific questions that can be answered by a "yes" or "no" or with a very short answer. For example:

- How long did the employee work for you?
- Was his or her work: __poor,__average or __excellent?
- Why did the employee leave your employment?
- Also make sure that you include a self-addressed stamped envelope for their reply.

After you have verified the information on all your applicants, you're ready to make your selection. The right employee can help you make money. The wrong employee will cost you much wasted time and materials and may even drive away your customers. Be sure that, once you've decided on the most appropriate applicant, you document in writing why you selected a specific applicant and why you did not select other applicants. Make sure that all decisions and comments are relative to job requirements and not other factors. Then, if you're challenged about your fair employment practices, you have the documentation that will keep you from being sued or paying large fines.

Setting Wages

Pay administration, which consists of defining jobs and appropriate pay, is a management tool that enables you to control personnel cost, increase employee morale and reduce workforce turnover. A formal pay system provides a means of rewarding individuals for their contributions to the success of your firm while making sure that your firm receives a fair return on its investment in employee pay.

If you're hiring union members, the local labor union will assist you in defining job descriptions and establishing pay levels and incentives.

There are two good reasons to establish a fair employee pay plan: your business and your employees. A formal pay plan, one that lets employees know where they stand and where they can go as far as take-home pay is concerned, won't solve your employee relations problems. It will, however, remove one of those areas of doubt and rumor that may keep your workforce anxious and unhappy—and less loyal and more mobile than you'd like them to be.

What's in it for you? Let's face it: in a mail order business good employees can make the difference between success and failure. And good employees are those who are happy and secure. Many people enjoy a good mystery, but not when it concerns how their pay is established. Employees under a pay plan can see that it's fair and consistent, and not at the whim of the owner. They are secure in knowing what to expect and what they can hope to earn in the future. So a good pay plan will help you recruit, keep and motivate employees. It can help you build a solid foundation for a successful business.

Minimizing Overtime

As your mail order business grows, employee overtime may be needed to get orders filled and shipped. Before the issue of overtime comes up, consider your employment policy or union requirements regarding payment for overtime hours. Depending on the standard workday and the number of hours required beyond that day, overtime can typically cost from 25 to as much as 200 percent more than standard pay.

In addition, efficiency decreases as overtime increases. By how much? One source has developed a table of overtime efficiency rates that, with five 10-hour days on the same job, the efficiency rate for the last two hours of the day is reduced to 87.5 percent. With five 12-hour days on the same job, the efficiency rate for the last four hours of the day is reduced to 75 percent. If the worker of five 12-hour days must move to another job after eight hours, the efficiency rate for the four hours at the second job drops to 68.8 percent. The point is that employee costs go up and efficiency goes down during overtime.

If overtime is required during busier sales seasons, make sure that you consider the costs of both overtime pay and reduced efficiency as you estimate your labor costs. Also, make sure that your employee handbook communicates your policies regarding overtime.

Understanding and Paying Taxes

Like it or not, the government is your business partner. And, as your partner, it receives a portion of your profits—even before you do. However, government can also help you make a profit through the Small Business Administration, Department of Commerce, state corporate divisions and numerous other business services.

The owner-manager of a mail order business plays two roles in managing taxes. In one role, you're a debtor. In the other, an agent or tax collector, whether you want to be or not.

As a debtor, you're liable for various taxes and you pay them as part of your business obligations. For example, each year you owe federal income taxes, which you pay out of the earnings of your business. Other tax debts include state income taxes and real estate taxes.

As an agent, you collect various taxes and pass the funds on to the appropriate government agency. If you have employees, you deduct federal income, Social Security insurance or FICA taxes, and, in some states, you collect state income taxes from the wages of your employees. If your state requires sales tax on your mail order business, you will collect it from your customers.

If you are a proprietor, you pay your income tax as any other individual citizen. Your income, expenses and profit or loss are calculated on Schedule C, which is filed with your annual Form 1040. A partnership files its own tax forms and passes the profits on to the partners for filing on their personal income tax forms. A corporation files on IRS Form 1120 or short form 1120A. Sub-Chapter S corporations file on IRS Form 1120S. Self-employment tax (Social Security and Medicare insurance for the self-employed) is reported on your IRS 1040 form using Schedule SE.

Individual proprietors and partners are required by law to pay the federal income tax and self-employment tax liability on a pay-as-you-go basis. That is, you file a Declaration of Estimated Tax (Form 1040 ES) on or before April 15, then make payments on April 15, June 15, September 15 and January 15.

Income tax returns from a corporation are due on the 15th of the third month following the end of its taxable year, which may or may not coincide with the calendar year. To find out more about your tax obligations, contact your regional IRS office (or call 1-800-829-3676) for the following publications:

IRS Publications

- *Tax Guide for Small Business* (Publication 334)
- *Guide to Free Tax Services* (Publication 910)
- *Your Federal Income Tax* (Publication 17)
- *Employer's Tax Guide* (Circular E)
- *Taxpayers Starting a Business* (Publication 583)
- *Self-Employment Tax* (Publication 533)
- *Retirement Plans for the Self-Employed* (Publication 560)
- *Tax Withholding and Estimated Tax* (Publication 505)
- *Business Use of Your Home* (Publication 587)

In addition, there are a number of federal forms you'll need for good recordkeeping and accurate taxation:

- Application for Employer Identification Number (Form SS-4) if you have employees
- *Tax Calendars* (Publication 509)
- Employer's Annual Unemployment Tax Return (Form 940)
- Employer's Quarterly Federal Tax Return (Form 941)
- Employee's Withholding Allowance Certificate (W-4) for each employee
- Employer's Wage and Tax Statement (W-2) for each employee
- Reconciliation/Transmittal of Income and Tax Statements (W-3)
- Instructions for Forms 1120 and 1120A for corporate taxes

The first publication on this list is the most important—*Tax Guide for Small Business*. Request it as soon as you begin planning your business. It describes business organization, assets, profits, net income, taxes and tax forms in clear language. It also includes sample tax forms filled in to illustrate how they are completed. A new edition is published each January about the prior tax year including important changes in the federal tax laws. Your state may have a similar publication for filing state business taxes.

Action Guidelines

As you can see, there are many responsibilities to managing the day-to-day operation of your mail order business. They include controlling operating costs, keeping useful records, offering quality mail order products at fair prices, managing employees and paying required taxes. Here are some things you can do today to apply what you've learned in this important chapter.

✔ Estimate your mail order business's operating costs.

✔ Develop an estimated operating budget for your mail order business including sales, costs and profit.

✔ Design or select a simple recordkeeping system, including journals and ledgers or accounting software.

✔ If you plan to hire employees, establish a payroll system.

✔ Set up equipment records and keep them off-site.

✔ Establish your business's hourly rate and develop your price list.

✔ List ways you can sell value over price.

✔ Establish a simple but usable time management system.

✔ Call the IRS toll-free number to order appropriate booklets and forms.

MARKETING YOUR
MAIL ORDER BUSINESS

What is your mail order business's market? A market is simply the group of prospective customers who would most benefit from your services. The market for your mail order business is made up of those who potentially could benefit from your products and services—a very broad definition that will apply to you and to your competitors. Defining *your* mail order business's market means determining the characteristics of those who would most benefit from your unique combination of products, knowledge, skills and resources.

This chapter will help you define your market and help you efficiently reach it.

The Purpose of Marketing

The first step to defining your market is to define who you represent to them. Because there are dozens of types of mail order business owners—and hundreds of potential markets—we will use broad examples. But you'll quickly get the idea and be able to apply it to your specialty.

For example, how would you define the market for a mail order business that sold booklets on how to raise prizewinning vegetables? That's who you are to your prospects. A prospect for this service is someone who grows or wants to grow vegetables, especially vegetables that can earn them acclaim. You have knowledge and experience in growing such vegetables. You've written down instructions so that others can do so. You know that, if your customers follow your advice exactly, they too can grow prizewinning plants. In fact, you can guarantee it. By defining the unique benefits, you can best define your prospects or market.

Here's another example of how successful mail order businesses market. One business owner decided that there were already too many mail order flower seed companies selling to individuals, so she decided to market exclusively to businesses. She found a seed wholesaler that offered wildflower seed packets that could be imprinted at a reasonable cost. She then developed a mail order campaign directed at businesses who wanted to improve goodwill with their customers. The companies could purchase and distribute wildflower seed packs with their name and message imprinted on it.

To market her service, she purchased a mailing list of businesses that buy promotional products. She then developed a mailer that reached the needs of these prospects, explaining why imprinted seed packs were an excellent and cost-effective promotional tool. Eventually, she included testimonials from satisfied customers.

Obviously, how your mail order business approaches your prospects will be somewhat different. Yet the principles will be the same. You will first determine whether there is sufficient opportunity for you to build your business and whether potential competitors are already adequately serving this market. Then you will focus your attention and your marketing on those who can best use your products.

Who are your prospects? They are those who have been influenced by your advertising as well as those recommended to you by satisfied customers. They are former customers, newcomers to the field, customers who need immediate help and your competitors' dissatisfied customers. They are people who have never before purchased by mail as well as those who buy most needed products by mail.

Some start-up mail order businesses begin by serving customers who cannot be served by the mail order owner's current or former employer. By working with them, these business owners reduce the amount of marketing they must do to develop customers. Most start-up mail order businesses then pay a marketing fee or a finders fee to these sources (their own former employers). It's another reason to maintain a good relationship with all of your past and current employers.

Let's look more closely at specifics on how to develop a profitable market for your mail order business.

Marketing Your Services

Marketing is a science. It's not a perfect science where the answer to a question is always the same. It's a science based on data, information, knowledge and wisdom. Data is easy to get and build into information. From this information comes knowledge and, eventually, wisdom. Wisdom is what makes your business profitable. Marketing builds your business.

The purpose of marketing is to get more customers. That's it. If you're new to business, the purpose is to get your first customers. If you've established a substantial business, the purpose is to keep those customers that you have.

There are dozens of ways that you can market your services to prospects and customers. They include the many forms of advertising, as well as literature, direct mail and telephone marketing.

Defining Your Customers

Customers are vital to your business. That's obvious. The better quality of customers, the greater the success of your business.

Who needs products or services by mail? Prospects for your mail order business include those who cannot find your product elsewhere, those who cannot shop at retail stores, those who prefer to shop by mail and many others.

There are two ways of defining prospective customers or prospects: demographics and psychographics.

Demographics is a study of statistics about people: where they live, how much they make, how they buy, their favorite brands. Retailers use census information to build demographics that help them in deciding where to build a store. Mail order businesses can use demographics, too. They can learn who would use their products and, then, where to find them.

As an example, if your prospects are those who collect expensive porcelain figurines you may be able to define them demographically as living within specific communities or earning above a specified income. This and additional information is available from a number of sources including list brokers.

Psychographics is the study of why people buy. You would think that most people buy for logical reasons. However, even in the business world, people often buy for emotional reasons and justify their decision with logical reasons. Some of these factors include lifestyle, religion and political persuasion. Knowing why your customers buy will help you sell to them more effectively.

If you've built a solid reputation in your field as a mail order enterprise that offers quality, you can sell that name. People want to go with a winner, so you will get some jobs just because people know you were involved. So learn what makes your customers buy and help them to buy from you.

Understanding your customers is so important that large corporations spend millions of dollars annually on market research. Although some formal research is important, a small business can usually avoid this expense. Typically, the owner or manager of a small mail order business closely understands the needs and buying habits of prospective customers. From this foundation, understanding your customers can be built by systematic effort.

Understanding buyers starts with the realization that they purchase benefits rather than products or services. Consumers don't select toothpaste. Instead, some will pay for a decay preventive. Some seek pleasant taste. Others want bright teeth. Or perhaps any toothpaste at a bargain price will do.

Similarly, industrial purchasing agents are not really interested in drills. They want holes. They insist on quality appropriate for their purposes, reliable delivery, safe operation and reasonable prices. Video games are fun. Cars are visible evidence of a person's wealth, lifestyle or self-perceptions.

You must find out, from their point of view, what customers are buying—and why. Understanding your customers enables you to profit by providing what buyers seek: satisfaction.

So, people don't buy products by mail. They purchase convenience, quality, uniqueness and related benefits. They couldn't care less about buying products by mail! Put yourself in their shoes and

and reread every direct mail piece that comes in your mail. What are they saying and how are they saying it? What can you learn and apply?

If you decide to hire a copywriter, ask for credentials and samples, then question him or her about the credentials and samples to make sure they are accurate. Give a short writing test to each candidate to make sure the copywriter can do the work. Finally, give a paid assignment to the top candidates.

Special Offers

You can increase how much you sell by mail by using inserts, premiums and easy-to-use order forms. Each element gives you the opportunity of increasing the response rate and total sales on your offer.

Inserts range from folders and booklets to brochures and circulars. These inserts should differ from other package components to catch the reader's attention. The more creative your inserts are, the better. Also include product and promotion inserts with the ordered products you ship.

A premium is an effective tool for boosting response to your offer. Front-end premiums are free gifts or samples sent with your direct mail piece, such as a coin. Back-end premiums are sent to people who respond to your mailing. Popular premiums include an "early bird special," a free gift or discount if the order is received by a specific date. Make sure the premium has a stated value and is useful to the prospect.

An effectively written order form can be an important part of the sales effort. Order forms should be easily recognizable, easy to complete and, if possible, personalized. A successful order form must include the price, the duration of the offer, terms of payment, delivery and processing time and any guarantees or warranties.

Telephone Sales

Mail order companies that take orders by telephone will need to focus special efforts on making the call a pleasant experience for the prospect. It is also an opportunity to learn more about your buyers and their needs.

The prospect wants to know:

- Why should I buy from you?
- Is your mail order business trustworthy?
- Are your products of greater value than the price?
- Do you have other products that I can benefit from?

You want to know:

- What's your name and how can I contact you?
- How did you hear about my business?
- What do you need to know to place an order today?

Learn all that you can from the customer. It not only develops a bond, but also establishes that you are a good listener—an important characteristic for success. In addition, you'll learn what other products and services you can also sell to your customers.

Personalized Sales

Advances in technology have revolutionized the way Americans learn about and shop for products and services. Reaching customers through direct mail can be accomplished by personalizing letters and envelope addresses. These elements can be personalized, semipersonal or generic depending on your product and marketing budget.

One of the most common methods of reaching prospective buyers is through personalized direct mail. When potential customers receive personalized mailings, they generally believe that the sender has used special thought and care in selecting their names. Recipients tend to think that not everyone on the block received the same letter. Many companies have found that personalizing their mailings increases the response rate by half.

The goal of personalized direct mail is to tailor your piece to the customer's preferences—much of which can be determined based on the list you use. Find out as much as you can about your customer and incorporate this information into any direct mail that you send.

If possible, use an individual's name and title when mailing to businesses. This not only makes your piece more personalized, but it can ensure that, if the addressee moves to another job, the replacement receives your offer.

Besides personalizing a direct mail piece with the recipient's name (and title), you can also use computer-simulated handwriting, preprinted signatures on letters and other components to make readers know that you recognize they are individuals.

It is sometimes difficult to fully personalize a direct mail promotion. An option is to semipersonalize the salutation by identifying the reader as the member of a select group. For example, "Dear Volkswagen owner," "To our Gold Key Customers," or "Dear software user" can help focus the reader on their role in reading your direct mail piece.

If your promotion crosses many prospect categories, you can still be more personal than "Dear Sir or Madam." Instead, use "Dear Friend," "Dear Businessperson," "Dear Professional," or another salutation that makes readers feel like you understand their needs.

Buying and Selling Mailing Lists

Your "list" is one of your mail order business's greatest assets. This list includes prospects who may have the need and the money to buy your product(s) from you. How can you compile your mailing list? You can start from scratch and build your own, turn to a list compiler, rent one from a list broker or work directly with a list's owner.

As mentioned in Chapter 3, response lists are lists of people who have previously purchased by mail. They are proven mail order buyers. Compiled lists are of people that have one or more things in common with each other. Response lists will almost always outpull compiled lists, says NMOA chairman John Schulte. "A list of golfers that have purchased by mail order is better than a plain list of people who golf."

Direct mailers should consider their own in-house list more valuable than any other. However, many in-house lists are overlooked. Approaching your current customers with a new product, sale item or service will often prove more successful than targeting a whole new population.

List compilers are professionals who work with a variety of

resources to compile a customized list of potential customers. Depending on your budget, they can be retained as outside resources as-needed. As the direct mail list industry has grown, list compilers have become increasingly specialized. The more narrowly focused the list, the more specific you can make your message and product offering. If you are looking for a specific list, utilize a compiler specializing in your field of interest.

List brokers bring together the owners of lists and direct mailers looking for lists, typically for a 20 percent commission paid by the list owner. To help sell their lists, many brokers will analyze your offer and consult with you on how to improve its effectiveness. To find a list broker, check the yellow pages of local and regional telephone books under the heading of "Mailing Lists" and "Mailing Services." The NMOA (see Chapter 3) has a special report on using mailing lists that includes the names and addresses of over 100 list brokers, compilers and managers.

You can also exchange lists with other mail order businesses. They can even be your competitors. For example, a small mail order bookstore in Arizona trades prospect lists with a similar store in Massachusetts. The lists are customers who have not purchased from the company within the last 180 days. This trade not only gathers new prospects for each bookstore, it also encourages the bookstores to work their existing customers harder. Are there competing or noncompeting mail order businesses that you can trade mailing lists with?

There are three common formats for mailing lists. Select the one most appropriate for your mail order business.

Cheshire Labels. Cheshires are popular for larger mailing lists such as catalogs where speed is important. Cheshire labels are printed "four-up" or four across the page on nonsticky paper. The labels are cut and affixed using a Cheshire machine.

Peel-Off Labels. For smaller mailings or hand-labeled mailings, peel-off labels are easier to affix. They are more popular for letter-size envelopes and can be attached by machine or by hand. They are also more expensive than Cheshires.

Database Names. A list of prospects on computer diskette or magnetic tape can be incorporated into personalized letters and related direct mail documents. This process is called mail merge. They are more expensive to buy because, unlike Cheshires and peel-offs, they may be used more than once. They are also more expensive to use because of personalized printing. However, they typically earn a higher response rate because the offers are personalized.

How To Make Multiple Sales

Lose a sale if you must, but never lose a customer. This business adage points out that a customer has greater value to your mail order business than just one sale. A satisfied customer will buy more products per order and place more orders than one that is unsatisfied. If the customer is satisfied and needs what you sell again, you have a good chance of getting a repeat customer. You didn't have to go out and spend additional money on advertising or work extra hours to promote your business. Your quality of business promotes itself.

The best way to get repeat business is to ask for it. As you talk with your customers, ask them:

- Is there anything else I can help you with?
- Would you like us to offer related products?
- What related products do you expect to need in the coming year?

You can also build repeat business by continually trying to expand each sales opportunity. It is more productive to get more business from current customers than to find new ones. Some successful mail order businesses build repeat business by writing a monthly newsletter to all their customers with new information on the products they sell and how the customers will benefit from them. Other mail order businesses make ordering easier with automated order lines that use customer numbers to expedite the orders.

Earning referrals is one of the most powerful types of business promotion. A referral is simply having one of your satisfied customers sell your services to prospective buyers. The word of a trusted friend is much more believable to prospects than is the word of an unknown salesperson.

So how do you get your customers to refer prospects to you? You ask them to do so. In fact, it should be an automatic question that you ask: Is there anyone whom you know who may also need our products? Ask it right after you close a sale, as you answer a customer service request and—especially—whenever anyone compliments your mail order business. Imagine the following brief exchange:

> *"I really appreciate how quickly you shipped my order. Even though I ordered late, I received it right on time."*
>
> *"I'm glad to hear that. Is there anyone whom you know who may also need our fast service?"*

In addition, once your customer has referred others to you, many feel a stronger obligation to continue to use your services. It will not only help you grow your mail order business but will also help you keep the customers that you have.

Remember that 80 percent of your business will come from 20 percent of your customers. Find out *which* 20 percent and keep selling to them.

How To Advertise for Profits

The purpose of advertising is to tell your potential customers how they will benefit from buying from you. The best way to do so is to let your other customers tell your prospects about their positive experiences when buying from you. That's called word-of-mouth advertising and it's the most valuable type of advertising there is. Unfortunately, it is also the slowest to develop. Your first satisfied customer may, in conversations, mention your good service once or twice a month. After hearing that a number of times and if they are looking for your service, a prospect may call you for your service. By that time you may be out of business due to lack of work.

Mail order businesses must advertise. How much should you spend on advertising? Successful mail order businesses typically spend about 10 to 25 percent of their estimated annual sales on advertising and promotion. Mail order businesses with easy-to-understand products and easy-to-define markets will spend less on advertising than others.

Successful mail order business owners suggest that the majority of an advertising budget should be spent during months when business is typically slower. Rather than an ad budget of $250 a month, slow months may require a budget of $400 or more, while busy months will have a budget of $100. Long-term advertising, such as magazine display ads, require monthly payments.

Advertising is based on impressions. Every time that your prospect sees or hears your name, you make an impression. It may be something small like seeing a classified ad in a favorite publication or it may be receiving a full direct mail package from your mail order business. Each impression is cumulative. After numerous impressions, large and small, your prospect may bring your name into the possible source part of his or her brain. Then, when a legitimate need for your product arises, the prospect considers you as a supplier. Think about it. How many times did you see or hear about Honda or Mr. Coffee before you even considered trying their product. Probably dozens or even hundreds of impressions were made. And consider that any negative feelings about these products are also impressions.

The point is that you will need to positively impress your prospects many times and in many ways before they can be upgraded to customers.

Besides advertising, there are numerous ways you can make positive impressions on prospects. One successful mail order specialty auto parts company produced a short article on how to restore old cars. This article was offered free of charge to numerous collector car magazines as well as posted to online computer services. The end of each article identified the source of the information and how to contact the supplier. The business owner estimates he has received more than $50,000 in new business as a direct result of that how-to article.

In addition, mail order business owners can speak to groups on related topics. If your mail order business sells a writing course, speak to writing groups. If you sell collectibles by mail, speak to related hobby groups, especially at national events. Just remember that it must be informative, not just an opportunity to sell.

Of course, you can enhance word-of-mouth advertising by developing testimonials. That is, when you have a customer who expresses satisfaction with your service, you ask the customer to write you a testimonial letter. The letter will describe appreciation for the quality of your products as well as that of your service to customers.

Unfortunately, only a small percentage of those who say they will write a testimonial letter will actually do so. But the problem isn't sincerity, it's time. Most customers just don't have the time to write such a letter. So some mail order businesses offer to write a draft of the letter themselves and send it to the customer for approval. A well-written testimonial from a well-respected customer will be worth literally thousands of dollars in new business to you. You will copy it and include it in with your brochure, quote from it in advertisements, and pass it out to prospects. It will be one of your best forms of advertising.

To encourage satisfied customers and their testimonials, most mail order businesses establish and promote a policy of satisfaction guaranteed. The profits lost are usually replaced by the profits gained through this policy. It is a helpful persuasion tool when trying to close a sale.

Of course, make sure that you have a customer's written permission to use any testimonials you quote in advertising.

How To Write a Great Classified Ad

Classified advertisements in magazines are often the best way to build your mail order business. How well prospects respond depends on how well you write your classified ad.

The first step to writing a great classified ad is to read great ads. Go to a library and find a recent copy of magazines you will use to reach your prospects. Then find older copies of the same magazines, preferably at least one year old. By comparing recent and older classified sections, you'll discover which ads have run for awhile. If they have been in the publication for more than a year, they must be profitable for those who placed them.

Next, read these proven ads to learn why they have worked. They probably use words like *free information, valuable,* and *satisfaction guaranteed.* They are probably two-step or combination ads because one-step ads typically don't pay their way.

Finally, write your own great classified ad using what you've learned about successful ads. Make sure you include a key so you know which ad pulled each order. Many successful mail order companies use a fictitious suite number to identify the ad, such as 123 Main St., Suite 412. Once you've placed the ad and it is published, include a copy of it in your advertising notebook.

To ensure that your ads are always working hard, follow these two rules:

1. Change *one* element (price, terms, headline, bonuses, etc.) of each ad to learn what works best at increasing sales.

2. Once all elements are as good as they can be, stop making changes to the ad.

How To Design a Great Display Ad

As your mail order business grows, or if you're selling higher-priced products, you will use display ads. Display advertisements rely on graphic images as well as words to sell your product or service. The graphics may be an attention-getting typeface, a powerful photo or drawing, an order form or other visuals that move the reader through the four steps of a sale, which are:

- Get the reader's *attention.*
- Earn the reader's *interest.*
- Make the reader *desire* your product.
- Encourage the reader to take *action* and buy your product.

These four steps—attention, interest, desire, action, or AIDA—are the primary stages of all sales.

Because most display ads are larger and have more room to sell, one-step offers are more popular. You can frequently sell your mail order product directly from a display advertisement. In this case, your display ad will be designed and written to carry the reader through these four steps. The headline will gain attention, an illustration and related words will increase interest, a list of real benefits will develop desire, and a satisfaction guarantee or testimonial and an order form or ordering information will move the reader to action.

As with great classified ads, you can design a great display ad by learning from successful ads. Study the magazines you will be using to reach your prospects. Find out which ads have run a year or more and study them carefully to learn why they are profitable. Then apply what you've learned to designing your own great display advertisement. It's that simple.

NMOA chairman John Schulte reports that the only way to be absolutely sure if a specific ad change is making the difference is with split-run advertisements. A split-run ad will have two versions of the advertisement, each in half of the publications and each with a unique key number. Split-runs are not available from all publications. If so, the cost of the placement is higher than with a full-run ad. However, split-run advertising can be very helpful in testing the effectiveness of advertising elements.

Here are some other display ad tips from NMOA:

- Don't try to sell products for a price higher than that of other products in the same publication.

- Products marketed to consumers through print media should be priced at $20 or less—preferably under $10—or as monthly payments (four easy payments of $9.99).

- Talk with noncompeting advertisers to compare results and learn from each other's mistakes.

- Make sure you have a "100% Money-Back Guarantee" stated prominently in your display ad.

How To Get Free Advertising

There are many effective ways that you can advertise your mail order business at little or no cost. Exactly which methods you use depend somewhat on your specialization.

Once you have your business card printed, carry a stack of them with you wherever you go. Pass them out to anyone who may be or know a prospect. As you stop for lunch, put your business card on the restaurant's bulletin board. Do the same on the bulletin board at a local market if you stop for anything. All it costs is the price of a business card.

Many mail order businesses overlook one of the best sources of free advertising—publicity. As you start your business, write a short article or press release and give copies to your local newspaper, radio stations, shoppers and national trade publications. Include in it information about your business, such as owners, experience, affiliations, background, expertise, purpose of the business, location, target market and contact name.

You can promote your business and get free advertising by offering to write an expert's column on your field of experience in exchange for an ad in a trade publication.

If you're personable and would be comfortable doing so, offer to host a radio call-in talk show on your field of knowledge or a related topic. Or you can become a regular guest on someone else's talk show. The publicity will make you a local celebrity as well as an authority that others will consider as they make buying decisions.

Also consider establishing an award or scholarship at a high school, trade school or community college in your business's name. Not only will you be able to deduct the award as a legitimate business expense, you can also use the award to promote your business in the media.

One more proven idea—seek awards. Join professional and business associations, entering all applicable business contests. If you win any of them, from first place to honorable mention, use the award as an opportunity to promote your business through local and national media.

When should you seek free publicity?

- When your mail order business takes in its first dollar
- When you're ready to celebrate a company anniversary
- When you hire a new employee
- When you change or add a location
- When you introduce a new product or service
- When you take on a partner or incorporate
- When an employee earns a promotion or special award
- When your business is mentioned in another media

Newspaper Advertising

The majority of homes in the U.S. and Canada receive a daily or weekly newspaper or a shopper. Many mail order companies use the pages of national or regional newspapers to advertise their business.

From the advertiser's point of view, newspaper advertising can be convenient because production changes, if necessary, can be made quickly. Also, you can often insert a new advertisement on short notice, depending on the frequency of the publication. Another advantage is the large variety of ad sizes that newspaper advertising offers.

The disadvantages to newspaper advertising include the cost of a large ad, which is necessary to stand out among other large ads, the short-life, throwaway nature of a newspaper and the poor printing quality of newspapers. If you do decide to advertise in national or regional newspapers, establish a consistent schedule rather than a hit-and-miss advertising program. Most importantly, ensure that the program is realistically within your budget.

If there is sufficient savings, sign a contract for a specific number of column inches of advertising each year rather than a standard size. By doing so you are earning a discount as well as allowing for business fluctuations. Reduce the size of your ad when business is good and increase it when you need more business. Some contracts will allow you to change your ad as much as once a week while still earning a substantial discount.

Marketing by Computer

The newest frontier for direct marketing is the computer. Products and services are now marketed using various online services. All that's needed to shop online is a computer, a modem and communications software. The leading online services are America Online (800-827-3338), CompuServe (800-524-3388) and Prodigy (800-776-3449). Each has what could be called an electronic shopping mall with stores that sell to the public and deliver products using parcel delivery services. If you're curious, a mall site can cost $10,000 or more to start and a percentage of all sales.

Another increasingly popular though not quite as structured online service is the Internet, a loosely linked network of government, university and business computers that you can access. Though not ready for heavy traffic, it is now serving many small businesses with worldwide opportunities for sales. Until recently, getting on the Internet required extensive technical knowledge and a lot of wasted time. Today, the World Wide Web offers easier access to Internet servers using what are called home pages.

The key to the Web's power is its "browsability," called its hypertext features. Hypertext is what enables someone using a compact disk encyclopedia to read an article (for example, on Abraham Lincoln), click the cursor on a key word (such as *slavery*), then instantly have an article about that key word on the screen. The process is handled through a hypertext markup language (HTML), which is read and translated by your software. A public-domain program called Mosaic does the reading.

If you're interested in business opportunities on the Internet and other online services, contact them at the numbers listed above. All currently offer a link to the Internet.

Per-Inquiry Advertising

One proven method of reducing your advertising costs is to pay for your ads from the sales you make. If you watch cable TV very much, you've seen 60-second ads that offer a toll-free number for placing the order. The number is frequently the same for all ads on the cable station. That's because the station receives the orders and payment directly, then places the order with the manufacturer at an agreed-upon wholesale price, keeping the difference. In most cases, the manufacturer produced the ad and the station provided the commercial time. This is called *per-inquiry*, or PI, advertising. It's frequently used by television stations to fill commercial time not otherwise sold. However, PI ads are also seen in newspapers and on radio stations. They are even used by mail order companies to help defray postage by including noncompeting offers in all outgoing mail.

Per-inquiry ads must be coded to ensure that the source is identified and everyone gets paid. The code may be in the address or the telephone extension number or in the product name.

As your mail order business grows, read direct marketing trade journals to learn more about PI advertising and resources that can help you use it profitably.

Action Guidelines

Learning how to effectively market your mail order business can quickly separate you from your competition. Proven marketing ideas are offered in this chapter. To implement some of these ideas for your mail order business, take the following actions:

✔ Define your mail order business's market. Who are your prospects? Who needs and will buy your products?

✔ Start a database of prospective customers or referral sources.

✔ How and why do your prospective customers buy your products by mail? What are their expectations?

✔ Learn what your prospects have in common with each other. Do they read a specific publication or live in a certain type of neighborhood?

✔ Establish a low-cost advertising campaign for reaching your prospective customers.

✔ Find customers who will write testimonial letters for you or allow you to write them on their behalf.

✔ Carry a stack of your business cards wherever you go and post them wherever you can.

✔ Establish your own techniques for developing repeat and referral business as suggested in this chapter.

MONEY AND YOUR MAIL ORDER BUSINESS

M oney certainly isn't *everything*. However it is a convenient way of keeping score. In most cases you will be monetarily rewarded in relation to the service you provide to others. The more you help the more you earn. How much of that you keep depends on how well you manage your money.

The purpose of this chapter is to ensure that you gain and keep an appropriate amount of money for what you do. It covers profits, cash flow, credit, financing and other money topics.

Profit and Loss

Profit is simply the amount of money you have left over once you've paid all of your expenses. If you have more expenses than income, you have a loss. Pretty simple.

Of course, there's much more to profit and loss than numbers on paper. Your business can actually show a profit on paper yet not have any cash. In fact, many profitable businesses go out of business each year because of negative cash flow.

How can you keep the cash flowing in your mail order business? By keeping good records, watching expenses and tracking the flow of cash in and out of your business. Before we cover cash flow, let's see how successful mail order businesses set up and use an efficient money-tracking system.

Keeping Track of Your Money

As the owner of a mail order business firm, you need accurate information on a regular basis to ensure that your business is running smoothly. As a single-person firm, you may have all the information you need in your head. But as your firm grows, you will need some information daily, other information weekly and still other data on a monthly basis. Let's take a look at what you will need and when.

In order to manage your mail order business firm, you will want the following information on a daily basis:

- Cash on hand
- Bank balance
- Daily summary of sales and cash receipts
- Daily summary of monies paid out by cash or check
- Correction of any errors from previous reports

You can either prepare this information yourself, have an office employee prepare it for you or rely on your accountant. While daily records will not show you trends, they will help you get a feel for the level of business that you're doing. And you'll be able to spot problems before they become serious.

Once a week, you or someone in your employ should prepare a weekly report on your firm. While still not sufficient for long-term planning, weekly figures will help you make small corrections in the course your business is taking. Weekly, you'll want the following reports:

- Accounts receivable report listing accounts that require a call because they are more than 60 days past due
- Accounts payable report listing what your business owes, to whom and if a discount is offered for early payment
- Payroll report including information on each employee, the number of hours worked during the week, rate of pay, total wages, deductions, net pay and related information
- Taxes and reports required to be sent to city, state and federal governments

Your weekly reports should be prepared by the end of business Friday so you can review them over the weekend or early Monday morning.

Once a month, you will want to review a number of pieces of information that have accumulated through your daily and weekly reports but were too small to analyze clearly. Now that they are part of a full month, information about cash flow, accounts receivable, and other parts of your business make more sense—and can be more easily acted upon. Following are some of the reports and information you will want to see every month:

- Monthly summary of daily cash receipts and deposits
- General ledger including all journal entries
- Income statement showing income for the prior month, expenses incurred in obtaining the income, overhead and the profit or loss received
- Balance sheet showing the assets, liabilities and capital or current worth of the business
- Check reconciliation showing which checks were deposited and which were applied by payees against your business checking account, and verifying that the cash balance is accurate
- Petty cash fund report to ensure that paid-out slips plus cash equals the beginning petty cash balance
- Tax payment report showing that all federal tax deposits, withheld income, and FICA, state and other taxes have been paid
- Aged receivables report showing the age and balance of each account (30, 60, 90 days past due)
- Summary of Schedule C entries

Let's cover three of the most important documents you'll review monthly: your income statement, your balance sheet and your cash flow forecast.

Your Income Statement

An income statement (Figure 7.1, on page 132) is a detailed, month-by-month tally of the income from sales and the expenses incurred to

INCOME
Cost of Sales
    Opening Inventory
    Purchases
    Total
    Prepaid Expenses
    Ending Inventory
    Total Cost of Sales
Gross Profit

EXPENSES
    Owner's Salary
    Payroll
    Payroll Taxes
    Rent
    Office Equipment and Supplies
    Telephone and Utilities
    Insurance
    Depreciation
    Miscellaneous
    Total Expenses

NET PROFIT (before income taxes)

Figure 7.1: Income statement.

generate the sales. It is a good assessment tool because it shows the effect of your decisions on profits. It is a good planning tool because you can estimate the impact of decisions on profit before you make them.

Your income statement includes four kinds of information:

1. Sales information lists the total revenues generated by the sale of your service to customers

2. Direct expenses include the cost of labor and materials to perform your service

3. Indirect expenses are your costs even if your service is not sold, including salaries, rent, utilities, insurance, depreciation, office supplies, taxes and professional fees

4. Profit is shown as pretax income (important to the IRS) and after-tax or net income (important to you and your loan officer)

Your Balance Sheet

A balance sheet (Figure 7.2) is a summary of the status of your business—its assets, liabilities and net worth—at an instant in time. By reviewing your balance sheet along with your income statement and your cash flow forecast, you will be able to make informed financial and business planning decisions.

The balance sheet is drawn up using the totals from individual accounts kept in your general ledger. It shows what you have left when you pay all your creditors. Remember: assets less liabilities equals capital or net worth. The assets and liabilities sections must balance—hence the name. It can be produced quarterly, semiannually or at the end of each calendar or fiscal year. If your recordkeeping is manual you will be less likely to develop a frequently updated balance sheet. Many accounting software programs can give you a current balance sheet in just a couple of minutes.

ASSETS
Current Assets
    Cash
    Accounts Receivable
        less allowance for doubtful accounts
    Inventory
    Prepaid Expenses
Total Current Assets
Fixed Assets
    Land
    Building
        less allowance for depreciation
Total Fixed Assets
TOTAL ASSETS

LIABILITIES AND EQUITY
Current Liabilities
    Accounts Payable
    Owner's Equity
TOTAL LIABILITIES AND EQUITY

Figure 7.2: Balance sheet.

While your accountant will be most helpful in drawing up your balance sheet, it is you who must understand it. Current assets are anything of value you own such as cash, inventory or property that the business owner can convert into cash within a year. Fixed assets are, for example, land and equipment. Liabilities are debts the business must pay. They may be current, such as amounts owed to suppliers or your accountant, or they may be long-term, such as a note owed to the bank. Capital, also called equity or net worth, is the excess of your assets and retained earnings over the amount of your liabilities.

Breakeven Analysis

Breakeven analysis looks at the relationship between costs and sales. Breakeven analysis establishes your business's breakeven point, which is the point at which your sales generate exactly enough revenue to cover costs.

In general, sales made beyond the breakeven point produce profits; those made below result in losses. It's generally a good idea to recalculate your breakeven point monthly or quarterly. If your company is experiencing rapid growth, you should do it more frequently.

Because breakeven analysis can indicate how changes in sales or costs affect profits, it can be used to answer such questions as:

- How much sales volume is needed to cover costs?
- How will additional costs or sales affect profits?
- How will certain purchases affect fixed and variable costs?

To perform breakeven analysis, you need to be able to estimate your fixed costs and variable costs. You also need to understand such concepts as sales price per unit and contribution margin.

Fixed Costs

Companies bear certain fixed costs regardless of whether goods or services are sold or not. Fixed costs (Figure 7.3, on page 135) don't vary with sales volumes or output levels but remain relatively constant. Fixed costs include rent, leases, utilities, salaries, taxes and insurance.

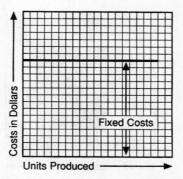

Figure 7.3: Fixed costs are used to calculate the breakeven point.

To enable you to keep the price of your goods relatively low, you want to keep fixed costs to a minimum. Low fixed costs can also make it possible to break even at lower sales volume or output levels. Conversely, if fixed costs creep upward, a company may have to raise prices just to continue to break even. This could make it difficult to price goods competitively. And in a worst-case scenario, a company that holds fixed costs too high might even price itself out of the market.

Variable Costs

In contrast to fixed costs, variable costs (Figure 7.4, on page 136) fluctuate depending on the number of units produced or the volume of sales made. Variable costs include the cost of goods sold, employees' hourly wages, commissions, bad-debt expenses and marketing and sales expenses.

An increase in sales usually results in an increase in total variable costs. As sales volume increases, however, average variable costs may actually decrease due to a more efficient use of resources. This is known as economies of scale, and it occurs primarily in manufacturing businesses.

One way to determine whether a cost is variable is to ask the question: Does the sale cause the cost? If the answer is yes, then the cost is variable.

One more point: The contribution margin is the difference between the average selling price per unit to the consumer and the average variable cost per unit to the company.

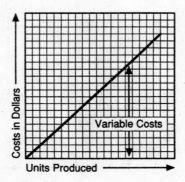

Figure 7.4: Variable costs are graphed to calculate a breakeven point.

Finding the Breakeven Point

The primary goal of breakeven analysis is to show the total amount of revenue a company must generate to reach its breakeven point. The breakeven point can be calculated by looking at costs in relation to either of two variables: total sales volume (sales volume method) or total units produced and sold (units sold method). Employing the first method, the breakeven analysis chart (Figure 7.5) looks at costs in relation to sales.

Sales Volume Method. To calculate the breakeven point in terms of total sales volume, use the following formula:

$$\text{Breakeven Point (Sales)} = \frac{\text{Total Fixed Costs}}{1 - \dfrac{[\text{Average Variable Cost per Unit}]}{[\text{Average Selling Price per Unit}]}}$$

The breakeven analysis chart (refer to Figure 7.5) assumes that a company is operated under the following facts:
• Fixed costs total $35,000.
• Average selling price per unit of $14.
• Average variable cost per unit is $9.10.

With the sales volume method, the breakeven point calculation is:

$$\dfrac{\$35{,}000}{1 - \dfrac{[\$9.10]}{[\$14.00]}} = \dfrac{\$35{,}000}{1 - .65} = \$100{,}000$$

This breakeven analysis shows that the company needs to generate $100,000 in revenue from its sales in order to cover its fixed and variable costs. The company's sales must surpass $100,000 before it will begin earning a profit. If the company's sales drop below the $100,000 mark, it will be operating at a loss.

Units Sold Method. The units sold method determines how many units a company will have to produce and/or sell to reach the break-even point.

Recall that the contribution margin is the difference between the average selling price per unit to the consumer and the average variable cost per unit to the company. This margin is what the company earns on each unit sold. It is not necessarily profit, however. Up until

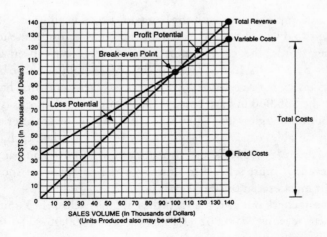

7.5: Example of a breakeven analysis.

the company reaches its breakeven point, the contribution margin on each unit theoretically goes toward paying fixed costs. When the company surpasses the breakeven point, the contribution margin then becomes the actual profit earned on each unit sold.

The formula for calculating the breakeven point according to the units sold method is:

$$\text{Breakeven Point (Units)} = \frac{\text{Total Fixed Costs}}{\text{Contribution Margin}}$$

For example, if you take the same numbers as in the previous example, you would calculate the breakeven point in units as follows:

$$\frac{\$35,000}{[\$14.00 - \$9.10]} = \frac{\$35,000}{\$4.90} = 7,143$$

This example shows that if the company prices its units at $9.10, each unit sold would have just paid for the variable cost of the unit. In other words, the contribution margin would have been zero ($9.10 – $9.10 = 0). In this case, the company would not have been earning any extra revenue to pay its fixed costs. Yet something has to pay for the $35,000 in fixed costs. What theoretically does this is the contribution margin—the $4.90 that the company makes after covering its variable costs. At some point, the $4.90 earned on each unit will add up to $35,000. As the calculation shows, for the company to break even, it must sell 7,143 units. For the company to show a profit, it must exceed this breakeven point.

We can check our arithmetic. If the company sells 7,143 units at $14 each, it earns $100,002 (7,143 × $14 = $100,002). So both methods came up with the same results: the company needs to earn $100,000 in revenues before it breaks even.

Calculating Potential Profit or Loss

By measuring the difference between total costs and total revenues (back to Figure 7.5, on page 137) and total sales or output you can calculate the company's potential profit or loss at any give sales volume or output level.

Look at the chart again. Notice that up until the breakeven point, total costs exceed total revenue. Total costs equal total revenue at the breakeven point. Beyond the breakeven point, total costs are less than total revenue. The relationships are now easier to understand. Apply these formulas for your own mail order business to track and manage income, costs and profitability.

How To Make Cash Flow in the Right Direction

Your business must have a healthy flow of working capital to survive (Figure 7.6, on page 140). Cash flow is the amount of working capital available in your business at any given time. To keep tabs on cash flow, forecast the funds you expect to disburse and receive over a specific time. Then you can predict deficiencies or surplus in cash and decide how best to respond.

A cash flow forecast (Figure 7.7, on page 141) serves one other very useful purpose in addition to planning. As the actual information becomes available to you, compare it to the monthly cash flow estimates you previously made to see how accurately you are estimating. As you do this, you will be giving yourself on-the-spot business training in making more accurate estimates and plans for the coming months. As your ability to estimate improves, your financial control of the business will increase.

Every time that you have to purchase on credit, you add interest costs to your business. If you had more cash you would be able to save more on interest expense. For this and other reasons, you can reduce your costs by increasing cash flow.

The cash flow forecast identifies when cash is expected to be received and when it must be spent to pay bills and debts. It shows how much cash will be needed to pay expenses and when it will be needed. The cash flow forecast enables you to plan for shortfalls in cash resources so short-term working capital loans—or a line of

Figure 7.6: Typical cash flow cycle.

credit—may be arranged in advance. Also, if you have excess cash, it allows you to put this cash to productive use and earn a return. It allows you to schedule purchases and payments so you can borrow as little as possible. Because not all sales are cash sales, you must be able to forecast when accounts receivable will be cash in the bank as well as when regular and seasonal expenses must be paid.

The cash flow forecast may also be used as a budget, helping you increase your control of the business through comparing actual receipts and payments against forecasted amounts. This comparison helps you identify areas where you can manage your finances even better.

A cash flow forecast or budget can be prepared for any period of time. However, a one-year budget matching the fiscal year of your business is the most useful. Many successful mail order businesses prepare their cash flow forecasts on a monthly basis for the next year. It should be revised no less than quarterly to reflect actual performance in the previous three months of operations and verify projections.

All businesses, no matter how small or large, function on cash. Many businesses become insolvent because they don't have enough cash to meet their short-term obligations. Bills must be paid in cash, not potential profits. Sufficient cash is therefore one of the keys to maintaining a successful business.

Mail order businesses face a continual cycle of events that may increase or decrease the cash balance. Cash is decreased in the acqui-

Gifts By Mail

Great Gifts for Great Friends

**123 Main St.
Yourtown USA
800-555-GIFT**

Cash Flow Forecast

DATE:	FOR TIME PERIOD:	APPROVED BY:
		PREPARED BY:

FOR INTERNAL USE ONLY	Date:		Date:		Date:	
	ESTIMATE	ACTUAL	ESTIMATE	ACTUAL	ESTIMATE	ACTUAL
Opening Balance						
Collections From Trade						
Misc. Cash Receipts						
TOTAL CASH AVAILABLE						
DISBURSEMENTS						
Payroll						
Trade Payables						
Other						
Capital Expenses						
Income Tax						
Bank Loan Payment						
TOTAL DISBURSEMENTS						
Ending Balance						
Less Minimum Balance						
CASH AVAILABLE						

Figure 7.7: Cash flow forecast.

sition of equipment or supplies. It is reduced in paying off the amounts owed to suppliers (accounts payable). Services are sold and these sales generate money owed from customers (accounts receivable). When customers pay, accounts receivable is reduced and the cash account is increased. However, the cash flows are not necessarily related to the sales in that period because customers may pay in the next period.

Mail order businesses must continually be alert to changes in working capital accounts, the cause of these changes and their implications for the financial health of the company. The change in the cash can be readily determined if you know net working capital and the changes in current liabilities and current assets other than cash.

> Let:
>
> | | |
> |---|---|
> | NWC | = net working capital |
> | CA | = change in current assets other than cash |
> | CL | = change in current liabilities |
> | Cash | = change in cash |
>
> Net Working Capital is the difference between the change in current assets and current liabilities:
>
> $$NWC = CA + Cash - CL$$
> $$Cash = NWC - CA + CL$$

This relationship shows that if we know the net working capital (NWC), the change in current liabilities (CL) and the change in current assets less cash (CA − cash), we can calculate the change in cash. The change in cash is then added to the beginning balance of cash to determine the ending balance.

Suppose you forecast that your mail order business income will increase $50,000 and the following will correspondingly change:

Receivables increase by $25,000

Inventory increase by $70,000

Accounts payable increase by $30,000

Notes payable increase by $10,000

Using net working capital of $48,000, what's the projected change in cash?

$$\begin{aligned}
\text{Cash} \quad &= \text{NWC} - \text{CA} + \text{CL} \\
&= 48{,}000 - 25{,}000 - 70{,}000 + 30{,}000 + 10{,}000 \\
&= -7{,}000
\end{aligned}$$

The answer is that, over this period of time, under the condition of increasing sales volume, cash decreases by $7,000. Is there enough cash to cover this decrease? This will depend upon the beginning cash balance.

At any given level of sales, it's easier to forecast the required accounts payable and receivable than net working capital. To forecast this net working capital account, you must trace the sources and application of funds. Sources of funds increase working capital. Applications of funds decrease working capital. The difference between the sources and applications of funds is the net working capital.

The following calculation is based on the fact that the balance sheet is indeed in balance. That is, the total assets equal total liabilities plus owner's equity.

Current Assets + Noncurrent Assets + Retained Earnings = Current Liabilities + Long-term Liabilities + Equity

Rearranging this equation:

Current Assets – Current Liabilities = Long-term Liabilities + Equity – Noncurrent Assets – Retained Earnings

Because the left side of the equation is working capital, the right side must also equal working capital. A change in either side affects the net working capital. If long-term liabilities and equity increase or noncurrent assets decrease, net working capital increases. This change would be a source of funds. If noncurrent assets increase or long-term liabilities and equity decrease, net working capital decreases. This change would be an application of funds.

Typical sources of funds or net working capital are provided by operations, disposal of fixed assets, issuance of stock and borrowing from a long-term source. The typical applications of funds or net working capital are purchase of fixed assets, payment of dividends, retirement of long-term liabilities and repurchase of equity.

How To Improve Cash Flow

As you can see, to grow your mail order business you need cash. Once you've analyzed cash flow and determined that you need more of it, what can you do? Depending on the specific type of business you own, you can find increased cash in your accounts receivable and in your inventory.

Accounts receivable represent the extension of credit to support sales. In your business, the types and terms of credit you grant are set by established competitive practices. As an investment, the accounts receivable should contribute to overall Return on Investment (ROI).

Excessive investment in accounts receivable can hurt ROI by tying up funds unnecessarily. One good way to judge the extent of accounts receivable is to compare your average collection period with that of rivals or the industry average. If your average collection period is much higher than your competitors' or the industry norm, your accounts receivable may be excessive.

If they are excessive, it may be that you're not keeping tight control of late payers. You can check this by developing an aging schedule. An aging schedule shows the distribution of accounts receivable with respect to being on time or late.

Failure to closely monitor late payments ties up investment and weakens profits. The more overdue accounts become, the greater is the danger that they will be uncollectable and will have to be written off against profits.

If the aging schedule does not reveal excessive late accounts, your average collection period may be out of line simply because your credit policy is more liberal than most. If so, it should translate into more competitive sales and greater profits. Otherwise, you should rethink your credit program.

Developing Your Business's Credit

Credit is simply a vendor's faith that the customer will keep a promise. You buy a computer system on credit, and the lender believes that you will pay back what you've borrowed—or, in the case of secured loans, you have assets that can be sold to cover what you've borrowed. So how do you build credit? Easy. You borrow a small amount, pay it back, borrow a larger amount, pay it back and so on.

A good way to start building your business credit is to use personal assets—signature, real estate equity—as collateral for your business. One enterprising mail order business owner simply applied for a credit card in his business name from the same company that sponsored his long-standing personal credit card. He asked for a small credit limit, used it and paid it off, then asked for an increased credit limit. Meantime, he used the credit card as a reference for a new account with a supplier. Other new business people use equity in their homes or investment land as collateral for credit with banks and suppliers.

Where and How To Get a Loan

"A banker is someone who lends you an umbrella when the weather is fair, and takes it away when it rains."

Where do mail order businesses get money to start or expand? A recent survey of small businesses reported that 23 percent had lines of credit, 7 percent had financial leases, 14 percent had mortgage loans, 12 percent had equipment loans and 25 percent had vehicle loans. For larger firms, the percentages about double in each category.

The ability to get a loan when you need it is as necessary to the operation of your business as is the right equipment. Before a bank or any other lending agency will lend you money, the loan officer must feel satisfied with the answers to these five questions:

1. What sort of person are you, the prospective borrower? In most cases, the character of the borrower comes first. Next is your ability to manage your business.

2. What are you going to do with the money? The answer to this question will determine the type of loan and the duration.

3. When and how do you plan to pay it back? Your lender's judgment of your business ability and the type of loan will be a deciding factor in the answer to this question.

4. Is the cushion in the loan large enough? In other words, does the amount requested make suitable allowance for unexpected developments? The lender decides this question on the basis of your financial statement, which sets forth the condition of your business, and on the collateral pledged.

5. What's the outlook for business in general and for your business in particular?

When you set out to borrow money for your firm, it is important to know the kind of money you need from a bank or other lending institution. Let's discuss loans and other types of credit. There are numerous types of loans available, all with their own unique name depending on the lender.

Signature Loan. A signature loan holds nothing in collateral except your promise to pay the lender back on terms with which you both agree. If your monetary needs are small, you only need the loan for a short time, your credit rating is excellent and you're willing to pay a premium interest rate because you're not using physical collateral, a signature or character loan is an easy way to borrow money in a hurry.

Credit Cards. Many a small business has found at least some of its funding in the owner's personal credit card. Computers, printers, books, office supplies, office overhead and other costs can be covered with your personal credit card. However, interest rates on credit cards are extremely high—sometimes double what you might pay on a collateral loan. But credit cards can offer you quick cash when you need it. If this is an option for you, talk to your credit card representative about raising your credit limit. It will be much easier to do so while you're employed by someone else.

Line of Credit. A line of credit is similar to a loan except that you don't borrow it all at once. You get a credit limit, say $50,000, that you can tap anytime you need money for business purposes. The most common is the revolving line of credit that you can draw from when business is off and pay back when business is good, providing that you don't exceed your limit. A line of credit is an excellent way for a mail order business to work through the ups and downs of seasonal business. With some restrictions, a line of credit can be established using a portion of your home equity as collateral. Using a secured equity earns you a lower interest rate.

Cosigner Loan. A cosigner loan should be one of the most popular loans for small businesses, but many business people never consider it. Simply, you find a cosigner or a comaker with good credit or assets who will guarantee the loan with you. If you have a potential investor who believes in your business but doesn't want to put up the cash you need, ask him to cosign for a loan with you. Your chances of receiving the loan are much better. Some cosigners will require that you pay them a fee of 1 to 4 percent of the balance or a flat fee; others will do it out of friendship or the hope of future business from you. In any case, consider this as an excellent source of capital for your new mail order business.

Equipment Leases. If you're purchasing equipment, computers or other assets for your business, the supplier may loan or lease the equipment to you. This often requires about 25 percent down so be ready to come up with some cash of your own.

Collateral Loan. A collateral loan is one in which some type of asset is put up as collateral; if you don't make payments you will lose the asset. So the lender wants to make sure that the value of the asset exceeds that of the loan and will usually lend 50 to 75 percent of asset value. A new mail order business owner often does not have sufficient collateral—real estate or equipment—to secure a collateral loan unless an owner uses personal assets such as a home.

Passbook Loan. Sometimes you can get a loan by assigning a savings account to the bank. In such cases, the bank gets an assignment from you and keeps your passbook. If you assign an account in another bank as collateral, the lending bank asks the other bank to mark its records to show that the account is held as collateral.

Life Insurance Loan. Another kind of collateral is life insurance. Banks will lend up to the cash value of a life insurance policy. You have to assign the policy to the bank. If the policy is on the life of an executive of a small corporation, corporate resolutions must be made authorizing the assignment. Most insurance companies allow you to sign the policy back to the original beneficiary when the assignment to the bank ends. Some people like to use life insurance as collateral rather than borrow directly from insurance companies. One reason is that a bank loan is often more convenient to obtain and may often be obtained at a lower interest rate.

Liquidate Retirement Funds. An option overlooked by many entrepreneurs is cashing out an IRA or Keogh account. The problem with this funding method is that money withdrawn is immediately taxable and subject to a 10 percent penalty for early withdrawal if you are under 59½ years old. However, this may be less expensive than a high-interest loan.

Borrow from a Retirement Plan. If you or your spouse are still working for an employer, you may be able to use your retirement plan as collateral for a loan to start your mail order business.

For more information on business credit, write to the Federal Trade Commission, Washington, DC 20580; Attn: Public Reference. Ask for their booklet *Getting Business Credit.* It's free.

Managing Interest Rates

Money is a commodity, bought and sold by lenders. Just like other products, you can often save money by shopping around. Following are some points to consider as you shop for money.

First, are there any loan fees or other charges required to set up or service the loan? Some lenders will require that a loan fee of 1 or 2 percent, or more, be paid in advance. Others will even roll the loan fee into the loan—so you actually pay interest upon interest. Others will deduct a monthly service fee from each payment as it is made. This arrangement is not necessarily bad; after all, the lender must make his profit from you in some manner. Just make sure that you understand what the actual cost of the loan is before you agree to it. You also need to know actual interest rates so you can compare rates between lenders.

Second, consider whether your best option is fixed rate or variable rate interest. Fixed rate interest means that the interest rate charged by the lender is the same throughout the life of the loan. Variable rate interest can vary during the term of the loan based on some outside factor. This factor is usually the cost of the money to the lender. Most variable interest loans have caps, specifying a maximum amount the rate can rise, both annually and through the life of the loan. The difference between the lender's cost and what he charges you is called the spread. From that spread comes his sales costs, office overhead, salaries and profit. The spread is also based on the amount of risk he is taking in loaning the money to you. Higher risk means a higher spread. There are numerous indexes used to establish the cost of money. Review all of the options with your lender, ask which one makes the most sense for your needs and get a second opinion.

Keep in mind that variable rate interest reduces the amount of risk the lender is taking, especially on long-term loans. He is virtually assured that, unless the money market goes crazy and goes over the cap, he will get his margin of profit from every dollar you send him. Lower risk means lower rates. The point is that you shouldn't disqualify variable rate loans from consideration. In many cases, they cost less than fixed rate loans and many lenders are more willing to make them.

To make sure that you pay the best interest rate available, don't jump into the arms of the first loan offer that comes to you. Shop around and compare. You may eventually decide to take that first offer but only because you've found nothing better.

Also, don't worry about getting the absolute lowest interest rate available. You may want to accept your regular lender's loan terms, even though it's a quarter of a percentage point higher, in order to maintain a mutually profitable relationship. That quarter point may only mean a few dollars to you and will reinforce your business relationship with your lender.

SBA Guaranteed Loans

The Small Business Administration has recently made sweeping changes to increase loan funds and reduce paperwork. One SBA official said, "What we're trying to do is get capital into the hands of people who have been capital starved."

The volume of business loans guaranteed by the SBA has increased from $3 billion in 1989 to approximately $9 billion in 1995. According to the SBA, the average loan was for $250,626 over a term of 11.5 years. About one-fifth of these loans went to companies that were less than two years old. Also important is that paperwork requirements for SBA guaranteed loans have been cut from as many as 40 pages to just 6 pages for loans over $100,000 and a single page for loans under that amount. Here is a summary of current SBA loan opportunities:

SBA 7(a) Guaranteed Loans. Private lenders make SBA 7(a) Guaranteed Loans, which can be guaranteed up to 80 percent by the SBA. Most SBA loans are made under this guaranty program. The maximum guaranty of loans exceeding $155,000 is 85 percent. SBA has no minimum size loan amount and can guarantee up to $750,000 of a private sector loan. SBA provides special inducements to lenders providing guaranteed loans of $50,000 or less. The lender must be a financial institution who participates with the SBA. The small business submits a loan application to the lender. After the initial review, if the lender cannot provide the loan directly, it may request an SBA guaranty. The lender then forwards the application and its analysis to the local SBA office. If approved by the SBA, the loan is closed with the lender, which disburses the funds.

SBA Direct Loans. SBA Direct Loans of up to $150,000 are available only to applicants unable to secure an SBA-guaranteed loan. Direct loan funds are available only to certain types of borrowers, such as handicapped individuals, nonprofit sheltered workshops for disabled workers, Vietnam-era veterans, disabled veterans, businesses in high-unemployment areas and owned by low-income individuals or for businesses located in low-income neighborhoods. The applicant must first seek financing from at least two banks in their area.

SBA Microloans. The newest SBA loan opportunity, microloans, is intended for smaller businesses who want to get started or grow and only need a few thousand dollars. There is $65 million in microloan money available to small businesses. The typical SBA microloan is for about $10,000, though the limit is $25,000 for worthwhile small business ventures. Contact your regional SBA office for additional information and requirements.

Loan Applications. If you're interested in applying for an SBA guaranteed or direct loan, call your regional office of the Small Business Administration. Even better, ask for the name of an SBA-certified lender in your area. The SBA loan program, notorious for its paper-work requirements, can be expedited by a lender that knows how to work within the system. You'll get your loan faster. In fact, those bankers that have preferred-lender status can handle your SBA loan without the SBA even being involved.

Offering Credit to Customers

Most successful mail order businesses are strict about a no-credit pol-icy. Most require cash or credit card payment with the order (Figure 7.8, on page 152). Those that do "carry their own paper" require that the customer complete a credit application (Figure 7.9, on page 153).

Using credit card services, such as Visa, MasterCard, American Express and Discover, can transfer bad debt problems to others and increase cash flow for your business. However, there is an initial setup cost and ongoing service charges. The credit card service will charge you a service charge of between 2 and 5 percent on each trans-action. Talk with your lender about offering your customers the option of paying for services with their credit card. It can dramati-cally increase sales for most mail order businesses.

Improving Financial Planning

Financial planning affects how and on what terms you will be able to attract the funding you need to establish, maintain and expand your business. Financial planning determines the human and physical resources you will be able to acquire to operate your business. It will be a major factor in whether or not you will be able to make your hard work profitable.

The balance sheet and the income statement are essential to your business, but they are only the starting point for successful financial management. The next step is called ratio analysis. Ratio analysis enables you to spot trends in a business and to compare its perfor-mance and condition with the average performance of similar busi-nesses in the same industry. To do this, compare your ratios with the average of other mail order businesses as well as with your own ratios over several years. Ratio analysis can be the most important early warning indicator for solving business problems while they are still manageable.

Gifts By Mail

Great Gifts for Great Friends

**123 Main St.
Yourtown USA
800-555-GIFT**

Order Form

Order Number:		Salesperson:

Telephone:	Ship Via:	Date:

Quantity	Description	Unit Price	Amount

TERMS

- [ ] Cash
- [ ] COD
- [ ] On Account
- [ ] MC / Visa / Amex - Card Number #
  Expiry date
  Name on Card

Subtotal	
Delivery Charge	
TOTAL	
% Sales Tax	
Balance Due	

Figure 7.8: Order form.

Gifts By Mail

Great Gifts for Great Friends

**123 Main St.
Yourtown USA
800-555-GIFT**

Credit Application

BUSINESS INFORMATION		DESCRIPTION OF BUSINESS		
NAME OF BUSINESS		NO. OF EMPLOYEES	CREDIT REQUESTED	TYPE OF BUSINESS
LEGAL (IF DIFFERENT)		IN BUSINESS SINCE		
ADDRESS		BUSINESS STRUCTURE		
CITY		☐ CORPORATION ☐ PARTNERSHIP ☐ PROPRIETORSHIP ☐ DIVISION/SUBSIDIARY		
STATE	ZIP PHONE	PARENT COMPANY _____ IN BUSINESS FOR		

COMPANY PRINCIPALS RESPONSIBLE FOR BUSINESS TRANSACTIONS

NAME	TITLE	ADDRESS	PHONE
NAME	TITLE	ADDRESS	PHONE
NAME	TITLE	ADDRESS	PHONE

BANK REFERENCES

NAME OF BANK	NAME TO CONTACT
BRANCH	ADDRESS
CHECKING ACCOUNT NO.	TELEPHONE NUMBER

TRADE REFERENCES

FIRM NAME	CONTACT NAME	TELEPHONE NUMBER	ACCOUNT OPEN SINCE

CONFIRMATION OF INFORMATION ACCURACY AND RELEASE OF AUTHORITY TO VERIFY

I hereby certify that the information in this credit application is correct. The information included in this credit application is to be used to determine the amount and conditions of credit to be extended. I understand that the other sources of credit considered necessary in making the determination may also be used. Further, I hereby authorize the bank and trade references listed in this credit application to release the information necessary to assist in establishing a line of credit.

SIGNATURE _____ TITLE _____ DATE _____

POLICY STATEMENT: INITIAL ORDER FROM NEW ACCOUNTS WILL NOT BE PROCESSED UNLESS ACCOMPANIED BY THE ABOVE REQUESTED INFORMATION.
TERMS: NET 30 DAYS FROM DATE OF INVOICE UNLESS OTHERWISE STATED.

Figure 7.9: Credit application.

One note before we get into ratios: members of trade associations often will share their balance sheet, income statement and management ratios with other members through studies and reports published by the association. It's just one more good reason to join one of the local or national mail order business trade associations. These percentages can help you in determining whether your mail order business is being operated as efficiently as other firms in your industry.

Important balance sheet ratios measure liquidity (a business's ability to pay its bills as they come due) and leverage (measuring the business's dependency on creditors for funding).

Liquidity ratios indicate the ease of turning assets into cash. They include the current ratio, quick ratio and working capital.

Current Ratio. The current ratio is one of the best known measurements of financial strength. It is calculated as follows:

$$\text{Current Ratio} = \frac{\text{Total Current Assets}}{\text{Total Current Liabilities}}$$

The main question this ratio answers is: Does your business have enough current assets to meet the payment schedule of its current debts with a margin of safety? A generally acceptable current ratio is 2:1; that is, twice as many current assets as current liabilities.

Let's say that you—or your lender—decide that your current ratio is too low. What can you do about it?

• Pay some debts.
• Combine some of your short-term debts into a long-term debt.
• Convert fixed assets into current assets.
• Leave in earnings or put profits back into the business.
• Increase your current assets with new equity (bring more cash into the business).

Quick Ratio. The quick ratio is sometimes called the acid test ratio and is one of the best measurements of liquidity. It is calculated as follows:

$$\text{Quick Ratio} = \frac{\text{Cash + Securities + Receivables}}{\text{Total Current Liabilities}}$$

The quick ratio is a much more exacting measure than the current ratio. By excluding inventories (typically small in mail order businesses), it concentrates on the really liquid assets with value that is fairly certain. It helps answer the question: If all sales revenues should disappear, could my business meet its current obligations with the readily convertible quick funds in hand?

A ratio of 1:1 is considered satisfactory unless the majority of your quick assets are in accounts receivable and the pattern of collection lags behind the schedule for paying current liabilities.

Working Capital. Working capital is more a measure of cash flow than a ratio. The result of the following calculation must be a positive number:

$$\text{Working Capital} = \text{Total Current Assets} - \text{Total Current Liabilities}$$

Lenders look at net working capital over time to determine a company's ability to weather financial crises. Bank loans are often tied to minimum working capital requirements.

A general rule about these three liquidity ratios is that the higher they are the better, especially if your business is relying heavily on creditor money or financed assets.

As a related indicator, the ideal ratio of gross revenue to working capital is 10:1.

Leverage Ratio. The leverage or debt/worth ratio indicates the business's reliance on debt financing (loans) rather than owner's equity. Here's how to figure it:

$$\text{Leverage Ratio} = \frac{\text{Total Liabilities}}{\text{Net Worth}}$$

Generally, the higher this ratio the more risky a creditor will consider lending you money. The ideal ratio is 1:1.

Net Profit Margin Ratio. Net profit margin ratio is a percentage of sales dollars left after subtracting the cost of goods sold and all expenses, except income taxes. It provides a good opportunity to compare your company's return on sales with the performance of other companies in the industry. It is calculated before income tax because tax rates and tax liabilities vary from company to company for a variety of reasons. The net profit margin ratio is calculated as follows:

$$\text{Net Profit Margin Ratio} = \frac{\text{Net Profit Before Tax}}{\text{Net Sales}}$$

Action Guidelines

Money is the root of all . . . *business!* It's not that business people are necessarily greedy. They just want some assurance that they will have enough money to continue their business—and their eating habits. Following are some proven ways you can make money and your mail order business can make long-term friends:

✔ Establish a simple system for keeping informed on the financial status of your business on a regular basis.

✔ Watch your balance sheet carefully and learn to apply ratios to ensure success.

✔ Keep a running cash flow forecast, no matter how simple, to ensure that money will continue to come in when you need it.

✔ Learn how to develop and use your net working capital rather than borrow from the bank.

✔ Keep your relationship with your banker open and friendly—just in case.

✔ Talk to your banker about becoming a credit card merchant.

GROWING YOUR MAIL ORDER BUSINESS

Industrialist Henry Ford once said that "coming together is a beginning, keeping together is progress, and working together is success."

This final chapter offers a collection of ideas and techniques from successful mail order business owners and other business people on how to make your business grow. It tells you how to manage employees, insure against potential losses for your business and your employees, manage risks and catastrophes and keep an eye on the future.

Managing Your Employees

A business is only as good as the people in it. Therefore, to effectively manage your mail order business, you must take the time to find and hire the right employees. The smaller the firm, the less it is able to afford the time and costs involved in hiring, training and firing the wrong employee.

How can you ensure that your mail order business will hire well? By setting and using proven personnel policies. Bigger companies have developed effective hiring techniques and procedures to lessen the risk. If you are going to successfully manage your operation, you too must apply some of these staffing techniques.

First, know yourself. Know what business you are in. Know your own personal abilities and weaknesses, and try to anticipate how you will deal with the situations that you expect to arise in the daily operation of your mail order business. Then, formulate your policies in writing. Include all matters that would affect employees, such as wages, promotions, vacations, time off, grievances, fringe benefits and even retirement policies.

You must establish employment and training procedures so that you have a better chance of getting the job done the way you want it done. Consider written policy decisions on the following:

Hours. Consider the number of hours to be worked per week, the number of days per week, evening and holiday work, and the time and method of payment for both regular and overtime work. Unnecessary payment of overtime at premium rates is a source of needless expense. By planning ahead, you may be able to organize your employees' work to keep overtime to a minimum. When peak periods do occur, you can often handle them by using part-time help paid at regular rates.

Compensation. Most or all of the employee's earnings should come from a base salary or wage competitive with the pay offered by other similar firms in your area. Depending on the job, it may be possible to supplement the base salary with an incentive, such as a small commission or quota bonus plan. Relate the incentive to both your goals and the goals of your employees. Whatever plan you use, be sure each employee understands it completely.

Fringe Benefits. There are numerous fringe or extra benefits you can offer employees as part of their total compensation package: discounts, low-cost or free life insurance, health insurance, pension plans, tuition reimbursement and club memberships.

Vacations and Time Off. Decide in advance how long vacations will be and when. Some businesses require that employees not take vacation time during the busiest times of the year. Also establish a policy for taking time off for personal needs, emergencies, holidays and other events.

Training. You must make sure that each employee is given adequate training for the job. In smaller mail order businesses, the training responsibility falls to the owner-manager. But, if you have supervisors, each one should recognize the importance of being a good trainer and of scheduling time to train new people.

Employee Appraisal

The majority of employees in the labor force are under a merit increase pay system, though most of their pay increases result from other factors. This approach involves periodic review and appraisal of employees' performance.

An effective employee appraisal plan improves two-way communications between the manager and the employee, relates pay to work performance and results, and helps employees understand job responsibilities and expectations and areas for improvement. An employee appraisal plan also provides a standardized approach to evaluating job performance.

Such a performance review helps not only the employee, but also the manager, who can gain insight into the organization. An open exchange between employee and manager can show the manager where improvements in equipment, procedures or other factors might improve employee performance. Try to foster a climate in which employees can discuss progress and problems informally at any time throughout the year.

To get the best results, use a standardized written form for appraisals. An appraisal form should cover the results achieved, quality of performance, volume of work, effectiveness in working with others in the firm and with customers and suppliers, initiative, job knowledge and dependability.

To keep your pay administration plan in tune with the times, you should review it at least annually. Make adjustments where necessary and don't forget to retrain supervisory personnel. This isn't the kind of plan that can be set up and then forgotten.

During your annual review, ask yourself if the plan is working for you. That's the most important question. Are you getting the kind of employees you want or are you just making do? What's the employee turnover rate? Do employees seem to care about the business? Most importantly, does your pay administration plan help you achieve the objectives of your business?

Employee Benefits

Employee benefits play an important role in the lives of employees and their families, and they have a significant financial impact on your business. Mail order businesses cannot be competitive employers if they don't develop a comprehensive benefit program. However, if not managed, an employee benefit program can quickly eat up a small firm's profits.

A comprehensive employee-benefits program can be broken down into four components: legally required benefits, health and welfare benefits, retirement benefits and perquisites.

Legally required benefit plans are mandated by law and the systems necessary to administer such plans are well established. These plans include Social Security insurance (FICA), workers' compensation insurance and unemployment compensation insurance (FUTA).

Health and welfare benefits and retirement benefits can be viewed as benefits provided to work in conjunction with statutory benefits to enhance employees' financial security. Health and welfare plans are perhaps the most visible of all the benefit program components. They include medical care, dental care, vision care, short-term disability, long-term disability, life insurance, accidental death and dismemberment insurance, dependent care and legal assistance.

Retirement plans are established to help ensure that employees are able to maintain their accustomed standard of living upon retirement. Retirement-benefit plans basically fall into two categories: *defined contribution plans*, which provide employees with an account balance at retirement, and *defined benefit plans*, which provide employees with a projected amount of income at retirement.

Perquisite benefits, or perks, are any other benefits an employer promises, such as a company automobile or truck, professional association or club membership, paid tuition, sabbatical, extra vacation, expense account, credit cards or financial counseling services.

Health and Welfare Plans

When purchasing a health and welfare plan, select an insurance professional whose clientele is made up primarily of small businesses. In fact, if you can find one in your area, select one that's used and recommended by other mail order business owners. Your insurer needs to be aware of the special problems that face small businesses, especially in your trade. Generous plans that look attractive and logical today may become a financial burden for your growing company. Remember that it is much easier to add benefits than it is to take them away.

Medical plans are usually the greatest concern of employers and employees. There are essentially two kinds of traditional medical plans. Major medical plans cover 100 percent of hospital and inpatient surgical expense as well as a percentage (typically 80 percent) of all other covered expenses. Comprehensive medical plans cover a percentage (again, generally 80 percent) of all medical expenses.

In both types of plans, the employee is usually required to pay part of the premium, particularly for dependents, as well as a deductible. Deductibles often range from $100 to $200 for single coverage and from $200 to $1,000 per person for family coverage.

A comprehensive medical plan is typically less expensive because more of the cost is shifted to the employee. Any plan you design should include features for containing costs.

As an alternative to a traditional medical plan, an employer may contract with a Health Maintenance Organization (HMO) to provide employees with medical services. The main difference between a traditional medical plan and an HMO is that the traditional plan allows employees to choose their medical providers while HMOs often provide medical services at specified clinics or through preferred doctors and hospitals. HMOs trade this flexibility for lower costs that are often passed on to the employee through reduced or eliminated deductibles or lower rates.

Disability insurance is an important but often overlooked benefit in small businesses. Disability insurance prevents a drain on financial resources to support a principal in the event that he or she cannot continue working.

Group life insurance is a benefit employees have come to expect in many regions and trades. Such insurance is usually a multiple of an employee's salary. Be aware that an amount of insurance over a legally specified amount is subject to taxation as income to the employee.

Employers who maintain medical and dental plans must provide certain employees the opportunity to continue coverage if they otherwise become ineligible through employment termination or other causes. In addition, if a firm's health and welfare plan discriminates in favor of key employees, the benefits to those employees are taxable as income. Talk to your plan administrator about current laws and requirements.

Retirement Benefit Plans

Retirement benefit plans are either *qualified* or *unqualified* plans. A plan is qualified if it has met certain standards mandated by law. It is beneficial to maintain a qualified retirement plan because contributions are currently deductible, benefits earned are not considered taxable income until received and certain distributions are eligible for special tax treatment.

Of the various qualified plans, profit-sharing plans, 401(k) plans and defined benefit plans are the most popular.

Profit-Sharing Plans. A profit-sharing plan is a defined contribution plan in which the sponsoring employer has agreed to contribute a discretionary or set amount to the plan. Any contributions made to the plan are generally prorated to each participant's plan account based on compensation. The sponsoring employer makes no promise as to the dollar amount a participant will receive at retirement. The focus in a profit-sharing plan, and in defined contribution plans, is on the contribution. What a participant receives at retirement is a direct function of the contributions. At retirement, profit-sharing plan participants receive an amount equal to the balance in their account. Profit-sharing plans are favored by employers because they allow employers the ability to retain discretion in determining the amount of the contribution made to the plan.

401(k) Plans. Another type of defined contribution plan is the 401(k). In a 401(k) plan, participants agree to defer a portion of their pretax salary as a contribution to the plan. In addition, the sponsoring employer may decide to match all or a portion of the participant deferrals. The employer may even decide to make a profit-sharing contribution to the plan. As described earlier, the focus is on the contribution to the plan. At retirement, participants will receive an amount equal to their account balance. Special nondiscrimination tests apply to 401(k) plans that may reduce the amount of deferrals highly compensated employees are allowed to make, somewhat complicating plan administration. The 401(k) plans are popular because they allow employees the ability to save for retirement with pretax dollars and they can be designed to be relatively inexpensive.

Defined Benefit Plans. In direct contrast to a defined contribution plan, a defined benefit plan promises participants a benefit specified by a formula in the plan. The focus of a defined-benefit plan is the retirement benefit provided instead of the contribution made. Plan sponsors must contribute to the actuarially determined amounts necessary to meet the dollar amounts promised to participants. Generally, benefits begin at retirement and are paid over the remainder of the employee's life, so a defined benefit plan guarantees a certain flow of income at retirement.

As a business owner, you can establish your own retirement plan, called a Simplified Employee Pension (SEP) plan. A SEP is a written plan that allows you to make deductible contributions toward your own and your employees' retirement without getting involved in more complex retirement plans. In fact, your SEP can include a salary reduction (elective deferral) arrangement to have part of your salary automatically transferred to the SEP retirement plan. Tax on this portion of your salary is deferred. The same program can be set up for your employees. Call the IRS for a booklet (*Self-Employment Pension Plans*, publication 560) on how to start and manage these plans. You will then file Form 5305-SEP, *Simplified Employee Pension–Individual Retirement Accounts Contribution Agreement*, with your federal taxes. It's a short form.

Selecting the Right Plan

Designing and implementing an employee benefit program can be a complicated process. Many small businesses contract with employee benefit consulting firms, insurance companies, specialized attorneys, or accounting firms to assist in this task. As you establish your program yourself or with a professional, ask yourself:

- What should the program accomplish in the long run?

- What's the maximum amount you can afford to spend on a program?

- Are you capable and knowledgeable in administering the program?

- What kind of program will best fit the needs of your employees?

- Should you involve your employees in the design and selection of the benefit program? If so, how much and at what stage?

Certain plans are more suitable for mail order businesses, based on the employer's financial situation and the demographics of the employee group. Employers who are not confident of their future income may not want to start a defined benefit plan that will require a specific level of contributions. However, if the employees are fairly young, a profit-sharing plan or 401(k) plan can result in a more significant and more appreciated benefit than a defined benefit plan. The 401(k) plans are very popular now that IRAs have been virtually eliminated. However, the nondiscrimination tests make it more difficult for small businesses to maintain 401(k) plans. If your work force is composed mainly of older employees, a defined benefit plan will be more beneficial to them but more expensive for you to maintain.

Remember that while a qualified plan has many positive aspects, the qualified retirement plan area is complicated and well monitored by the government. Make sure you have adequate counsel before you decide on the most appropriate plan for your business.

Managing Risk

You've learned how to increase sales and reduce expenses for your mail order business. But even as your business grows and profits, you can still lose money. How?

- An employee is injured on the job and sues you.

- An employee runs off with money stolen from your business.

- A fire or flood wipes out your office, equipment and important records.

- A partner in your business files bankruptcy and the courts attach your business.

- The local economy goes sour and you can't find enough work for six months or more.

- A business partner is involved in a divorce settlement and business assets must be sold to meet a court order.

- The IRS comes after you for a large tax bill they think you owe them and takes over your bank account until everything is resolved.

The list goes on. There are many ways that an otherwise profitable business can quickly be thrown into a situation where the business's future is in jeopardy. What can you do about it? First, you can make sure you understand the risks involved in your business. And, second, you can take precautions to ensure that the risks are minimal. They will never go away, but, through smart risk management, you can minimize them and prepare for the worst.

Identifying Potential Risks

Of course, the best time to minimize the risk of business disasters is before they happen. And the first step to minimizing risk is identifying the risks that can occur. Business risks that mail order businesses typically face are:

- Acts of nature (fire, flood)
- Acts of man (theft, vandalism, vehicle accidents)
- Personal injury (employee or user)
- Legal problems (liens, unfair trade practices, torts)
- Financial (loss of income, funding or assets)
- Taxation (judgments, tax liens)
- Management (loss of owner's capacity to manage)

Of course, every method of reducing risk—attorneys, insurance, binding agreements, security systems, fire alarms—cost money. So when is it more cost-effective to accept the risk rather than pay for products or services that eliminate the risk? It's a simple question with a simple answer—it all depends.

Actually, the best time to minimize risk in your business is right now. The real answer lies in balancing the cost of loss against the cost of security. As an example, if your work vehicle is a beat-up 1972 Ford van with a pinto paint job, collision insurance that costs an extra $300 a year is more expensive than absorbing the cost of body damage from minor accidents.

There are a number of ways that you can keep your losses to a minimum. They include preventing or limiting exposure to loss, risk retention, transferring risk and insurance.

One principle of loss prevention and control is the same in business as it is in your personal life: avoid activities that are too hazardous. For example, don't leave cash or valuable equipment where it can be easily stolen.

A mail order business owner may decide that the firm can afford to absorb some losses, either because the frequency and probability of loss are low or because the dollar value of loss is manageable. Maybe your mail order business owns an older vehicle and its drivers have excellent safety records, so you decide to drop the collision insurance on these vehicles but retain it on newer vehicles.

Insuring Against Risks

The most common method of transferring risk is purchasing insurance. By insuring your business and equipment, you have transferred much of the risk of loss to the insurance company. You pay a relatively small amount in premium rather than run the risk of not protecting yourself against the possibility of a much larger financial loss.

Of course, you can be overinsured or pay more than is necessary for the amount of risk that you transfer. That's why it's so important to select a reputable and professional insurance agent to advise you. But in business insurance, only you can decide which exposures you absolutely must insure against. Some decisions, however, are already made for you: those required by law and those required by others as a part of doing business with them. Workers' compensation insurance is an example of insurance that is required by law. Your bank probably won't lend you money for equipment, real estate or other assets unless you insure them against loss.

Today, very few businesses—and especially mail order business— have sufficient financial reserves to protect themselves against the

Business Insurance Tips

Here are some tips on buying common business insurance coverage.

Fire Insurance

- You can add other perils—such as windstorm, hail, smoke, explosion, vandalism and malicious mischief—to your basic fire insurance at a relatively small additional fee.

- If you need comprehensive coverage, your best buy may be one of the all-risk contracts—such as the $1 million umbrella policy—that offer the broadest available protection for the money.

- Remember that the insurance company may compensate your losses by paying actual cash value of the property at the time of the loss, it may repair or replace the property with material of like kind and quality or it may take all the property at the agreed or appraised value and reimburse you for your loss.

- Even if you have several policies on your property, you can still collect only the amount of your actual cash loss. All the insurers share the payment proportionately.

- Special protection other than the standard fire insurance policy is needed to cover the loss by fire of accounts, bills, currency, deeds, evidence of debt and securities.

- After a loss, you must use all reasonable means to protect the property from further loss or run the risk of having your coverage canceled.

- In most cases, to recover your loss you must furnish within 60 days a complete inventory of the damaged, destroyed and undamaged property showing in detail quantities, costs, actual cash value and amount of loss claimed.

- If you and your insurer disagree on the amount of the loss, the question may be resolved through special appraisal procedures provided for in the fire insurance policy.

- You may cancel your policy without notice at any time and get part of the premium returned. The insurance company also may cancel at any time within a specified period, usually five days, with a written notice to you.

Liability Insurance

- You may be legally liable for damages even in cases where you used reasonable care.

- Under certain conditions, your business may be subject to damage claims even from trespassers.

- Most liability policies require you to notify the insurer immediately after an incident on your property that might cause a future claim. This holds true no matter how unimportant the incident may seem at the time it happens.

- Even if the suit against you is false or fraudulent, the liability insurer pays court costs, legal fees and interest on judgments in addition to the liability judgments themselves.

- You can be liable for the acts of others under contracts you have signed with them, such as independent contractors. This liability is insurable.

Automobile Insurance

- When an employee uses a car on your behalf, you can be legally liable even though you don't own the car or truck.

- You can often get deductibles of almost any amount—$250, $500, $1,000—and thereby reduce your premiums.

- Automobile medical-payments insurance pays for medical claims, including your own, arising from vehicular accidents regardless of the question of negligence.

- In most states, you must carry liability insurance or be prepared to provide a surety bond or other proof of financial responsibility when you're involved in an accident.

- You can purchase uninsured motorist protection to cover your own bodily injury claims from someone who has no insurance.

- Personal property stored in a car or truck and not attached to it is not covered under an automobile policy.

Workers' Compensation Insurance

- Federal laws require that an employer provide employees a safe place to work, hire competent fellow employees, provide safe tools and warn employees of existing danger. Whether or not an employer provides these things, he is liable for damage suits brought by an employee and possible fines or prosecution.

- State law determines the level or type of benefits payable under workers' compensation insurance policies.

- Not all employees are covered by workers' compensation insurance laws. The exceptions are determined by state law and therefore vary from state to state.

- You can save money on workers' compensation insurance by seeing that your employees are properly classified. Rates for workers' compensation insurance vary from 0.1 percent of the payroll for safe occupations to about 25 percent or more of the payroll for very hazardous occupations.

- Most employers can reduce their workers' compensation insurance premium cost by reducing their accident rates below the average. They do this by using safety and loss-prevention measures established by the individual state.

hundreds of property and liability exposures that they face. What those exposures are, what their dollar value is and how much is enough are difficult questions. As you build a team of business professionals to help you effectively manage your business, you should use an insurance professional.

Four kinds of insurance are essential to your business: fire, liability, automobile and workers' compensation insurance. Selecting from among the dozens of available policies and options can be somewhat confusing to most business people. However, the following information will guide you in making the right decisions for the right reasons.

Dealing with Business Cycles

No businesses are truly recession-proof. All businesses have cycles where sales become easier or harder to make. Mail order businesses are subject to the same business cycle that most businesses face. Even so, there are steps you can take to minimize the market's downswing and extend its upswing.

First, determine the business cycle for your market. Reviewing income and financial records from prior years or checking with the local chamber of commerce, you can draw a chart illustrating the local business cycle. In your region, it may be that most of the market for your service occurs in the spring and summer. Or the cycle may be fairly equal across the year, but alternate years may fluctuate up or down. The first step to coping with recessions in the local business cycle is to determine exactly what and when that cycle is.

The next step is to begin planning for it. That is, if you're coming up to a typically slower period, determine what you need to do. In past years, how much has income dropped? For how long? Can you find income sources in other specialities where the cycle is moving up? What expenses can you cut? Do you have an employee who would like a seasonal layoff so he can catch up on other interests? Maybe you need to dramatically cut back on your expenses and debts for this period. If so, list them out now, determine which will naturally diminish and which will need to be reduced.

One successful mail order operator, while in a busy period, decided that times would be much slower six months hence. So he talked with his bank and other creditors, offering to prepay debts and expenses now so he could reduce payments later. It worked. When times got rougher, he reduced his expenses and weathered the problem.

If you aren't into your slow season yet, you can also talk to your lender about building a line of credit now that will help you get through the tougher times ahead.

Another source for cash to tide you through a recession is available from a second mortgage on your building, your home, or other large asset. Speak with your lender about this opportunity. Even if you decide not to take out a second mortgage, you will be ready if and when you need to do so.

Consider widening your market. That is, travel to a nearby metropolitan area and study whether you can expand your services to reach it. If so, you can pick up additional sales by either subcontracting your services or by promoting your services in the expanded market. It certainly beats starving at home.

Improving Collections

As many mail order businesses have learned, collecting money for products and services you've sold can be the most difficult part of business. However, many successful mail order businesses have developed proven methods for improving collections and enhancing cash flow. Here are some tips from these pros.

First, send out an invoice on the day the sale occurs. Depending on your recordkeeping system, you may be able to do it automatically.

Second, follow the invoice with a statement of all money owed on the account, current and past due. Many businesses send an account statement on the first of each month. However, others have been more successful by sending them out a few days earlier.

Third, if an account is 30 days overdue, send a polite and personalized collection letter. Be brief, be specific, be friendly. Offer to discuss any problems the customer has regarding the account.

Fourth, as needed, send out two more collection letters: one at 60 days and one at 90 days. Each one is more firm. The final letter should indicate that the next step is to turn the account over to a collection agency.

Fifth, if these actions don't work, call to settle the account. A collection agency will charge 25 to 50 percent of the account balance to collect it. If you can, offer to discount the account for quick payment.

Finally, if all else fails, turn the account over to a collection agency. As an alternative, you may decide to simply write the account off as a bad debt expense.

Many business owners allow bad debts to embitter them, making them skeptical of all customers. A better action is to establish a clear and easy-to-follow credit and collection policy that reduces losses while maintaining good customer relationships. An effective credit and collection policy can increase cash flow while reducing stress.

Advanced Expense Management for Mail Order Businesses

Every dollar saved in overhead is a dollar on the bottom line of net profit—and a dollar less borrowed.

The object of reducing costs in your mail order business is to increase profits. Increasing profits through cost reduction must be based on the concept of an organized, planned program. Unless adequate records are maintained through an efficient and accurate accounting system, there can be no basis for analyzing costs.

Cost reduction is not simply attempting to slash any and all expenses without order. The owner-manager must understand the nature of expenses and how expenses interrelate with sales, inventories, overhead, gross profits and net profits. Nor does cost reduction mean only the reduction of specific expenses. You can achieve greater profits through more efficient use of your expense dollar. Some of the ways you do this are by increasing the average sale per customer, by getting a larger return for your promotion and sales dollar, and by improving your internal methods and procedures.

As an example, one small mail order business owner was quite pleased when, in a single year, sales went from $40,000 to $200,000. However, at the end of the year, records showed that net profit the prior year, with lower sales, was actually higher. Why? Because the expenses of doing business grew at a rate faster than the income.

Your goal should be to pay the right price for prosperity. Determining that price for your operation goes beyond knowing what your expenses are. Reducing expenses to increase profit requires that you obtain the most efficient use of your expense dollars.

Checking job records, you might determine that one of your employees is significantly less efficient than other employees performing the same tasks. You can then reduce expenses by increasing this employee's efficiency through training. By watching this employee perform his or her job, you can determine where the inefficiencies are and help him or her to overcome them. If done with consideration for the person, he or she will appreciate your attention, and so will your profit line.

Sometimes you cannot cut an expense item. But you can get more from it and thus increase your profits. In analyzing your expenses you should use percentages rather than actual dollar amounts. For example, if you increase sales and keep the dollar amount of an expense the same, you have decreased that expense as a percentage of income. When you decrease your cost percentage, you increase your percentage of profit.

On the other hand, if your sales volume remains the same, you can increase the percentage of profit by reducing a specific item of expense. Your goal, of course, is to simultaneously decrease specific expenses and increase their productive worth.

Before you can determine whether cutting expenses will increase profits, you need information about your operation. This information can be obtained only if you adequately use recordkeeping and financial management systems discussed earlier.

Locating Reducible Expenses

Your income statement provides a summary of expense information and is the focal point in locating expenses that can be cut. For this reason, the information should be as current as possible. As a report of what has already been spent, an income statement alerts you to expense items that should be watched in the present business period. If you get an income statement only at the end of the year, you should consider having one prepared more often. At the end of each quarter is usually sufficient for smaller firms. Larger mail order businesses should receive the information on a monthly basis.

Regardless of the frequency, the best option is to prepare two income statements. One statement should report the sales, expenses, profit and loss of your operations cumulatively for the current business year to date. The other statement should report on the same items for the last complete month or quarter. Each of the statements should also carry the following information:

- This year's figures and each item as a percentage of sales
- Last year's figures and the percentages
- The difference between last year's and this year's figures—over or under
- Budgeted figures and their respective percentages
- The difference between current year actuals and the budgeted figures—over or under
- Average percentages for similar businesses (available from trade associations and the U.S. Department of Labor)
- The difference between your annual percentages and the industry ratios—over or under

This information allows you to locate expense variations in three ways:

1. By comparing this year to last year
2. By comparing expenses to your own budgeted figures
3. By comparing your percentages to the operating ratios for similar businesses

The important basis for comparison is the percentage figure. It represents a common denominator for all three methods. When you have indicated the percentage variations, you should then study the dollar amounts to determine what kind of corrective action is needed.

Because your cost cutting will come largely from variable expenses, you should make sure that they are indicated on your income statements. Variable expenses are those which fluctuate with the increase or decrease of sales volume. Some of them are overtime, temporary help, advertising, salaries, commissions and payroll taxes. Fixed expenses are those which stay the same regardless of sales volume. Among them are your salary, salaries for permanent employees, depreciation, rent and utilities.

When you have located a problem expense area, the next step obviously is to reduce that cost so as to increase your profit. A key to the effectiveness of your cost-cutting action is the worth of the various expenditures. As long as you know the worth of your expenditures, you can profit by making small improvements in expenses. Keep an open eye and an open mind. It is better to do a spot analysis once a month than to wait several months and then do a detailed study.

Take action as soon as possible. You can refine your cost-cutting action as you go along. Be persistent. Results typically come slower than you might like. Keep in mind that only persistent analysis of your records and constant action can help keep expenses from eating up profit.

Reducing Overhead

Business overhead is simply the costs of keeping your doors open. If your mail order business is located in your home, overhead costs are probably small. But if you have a shop, an office and office personnel, your overhead is greater. It's also large if you have high debt to banks, suppliers and investors.

The suggestion made earlier in this book was to start out small and let your growing business force you into larger quarters. That is, depending on your mail order business market, start with an office in a corner of your home. Then, as business grows, take on greater obligations for additional overhead. If you build the customer's perception of quality with your product, you won't have to maintain impressive offices. Few customers will decide not to do business with you because your office is in your home.

You can also reduce overhead by carefully watching the costs of supplies. Printed stationery is an excellent way to promote the quality of your business, but you don't need printed notepads unless the customer will see them. For the price of generic ink pens you can often get ones that include your business name and phone number. But don't buy so many that they wind up costing more than quality ink pens because you've changed your address or phone number. Buy supplies in quantity if you can, but don't buy more than you will use in three to six months unless you're certain that they won't become out-of-date.

Travel expenses can easily get out of hand without good record-keeping. That means developing a simple system for tracking transportation, lodging, meals, phone and other costs.

Labor costs is one place where the profits of a small mail order business can quickly be eaten away. Don't hire an office manager or secretary until you absolutely must. It's more profitable to do the required filing and office functions yourself after normal business hours or on weekends. Or you can ask the help of a spouse or older child who could be put on the payroll as soon as your business can afford it.

Some small mail order businesses use temporary help or outside services rather than hire employees and all deal with the taxes and records that come with them. They have records kept by a bookkeeping or accounting service, office cleaning is done by a janitorial service (or the boss), telephones are answered by an answering service, correspondence and retyping service is performed by a secretarial service. Order fulfillment that the owner can't handle is contracted out to other mail order businesses. They know that the complexity of regulations and taxation is endlessly multiplied when the first employee is hired—so they avoid hiring anyone until their success requires them to do so.

Long-distance phone calls can quickly add to your expenses and cut into your profits—especially when they are personal calls made by employees. Many successful mail order businesses use a telephone call record to keep track of long-distance calls, then compare the report with the monthly phone bill. Calls not listed on the report are assumed to be personal calls and should be checked out.

Keeping an Eye on the Future

As your mail order business grows, there are many new elements to your task of managing a successful business. You must consider and plan for the loss of a key person in the business structure. You must remind yourself to enjoy what you're doing. You must review your options if the business fails. You must consider the long term and begin planning for retirement. Planning well for tomorrow can reduce your worries today.

Succession in a Proprietorship

The personal skills, reputation and management ability of the sole proprietor help to make the business successful. Without these life values the business is worth only the liquidation value of the tangible assets.

The sole proprietor's personal and business assets are one and the same. When a proprietor dies, the loss can become a financial disaster to the estate and the business. The business that was producing a good living for the owner and family will become a defunct business. What are the options?

The business may be transferred to a capable family member as a gift through provisions in the proprietor's will or by a sale provided through a prearranged purchase agreement effective at death. Cash is needed to offset losses to the business caused by the owner's death, to equalize the value of bequests made to other family members if the transfer is a gift and to provide the sale price if the transfer is through sale.

If the buyer is a key employee, competitor or third party, the business may be transferred at death, based on a prearranged sale agreement. However, cash is needed to provide a business continuation fund to meet expenses and perhaps to offset losses until the business adjusts to the new management.

If future management is not available then the business must be liquidated. Cash is needed to offset the difference between the business's going-concern value and its auction-block liquidation value, to provide a fund for income replacement to the family and to pay outstanding business debts.

Succession in a Partnership

Unless there is a written agreement to the contrary, the death of a partner automatically dissolves the firm. In the absence of such an agreement, surviving partners have no right to buy the deceased's partnership interest. Surviving partners cannot assume the goodwill or take over the assets without consent of the deceased partner's estate. If the deceased was in debt to the partnership, the estate must settle the account in full and in cash.

The surviving partners act as liquidating trustees. They have exclusive possession of firm property but no right to carry on the business. If the business is continued, the surviving partners must share all profits with the deceased partner's estate and are liable for all losses. They must convert everything into cash at the best price obtainable. They must make an accounting to the deceased's estate and divide the proceeds with the estate. They must liquidate themselves out of their business and income.

What are the options a business has on the death of a partner?

If the surviving partner and deceased's heirs do nothing, the business is liquidated, resulting in auction-price value for the salable assets. The business may receive nothing for goodwill. This is a disastrous solution for both the deceased partner's family and the surviving partners. It means termination of jobs for the surviving partners and employees.

The surviving partners may attempt to reorganize the partnership by taking the heirs into the partnership. But if heirs are unable to work in the business, the surviving partners must do all the work and share the profits. They could accept a new partner picked by the heirs. The surviving partners could also sell their interest in the business to the heirs or conversely, buy out the heirs' interest.

Of course, there are some preparations that can be made prior to the death of a partner that will make a reorganization smoother. Buy and sell agreements funded with life insurance should be entered into while all partners are alive. Such an agreement, drafted by an attorney, will typically include a commitment by each partner not to dispose of his or her interest without first offering it at an agreed sale price to the partnership. The agreement will also include a provision for the partnership to buy a deceased partner's interest. The funding of the purchase will typically be from the proceeds of a life insurance policy written for that specific purpose.

Succession in a Corporation

The death of a stockholder who has been active in the operation of a closely held corporation allows the business entity to continue its legal structure but not its personal structure. The interests of the heirs of the deceased inevitably come in conflict with the interests of the surviving associates.

What options are available to surviving stockholders?

The deceased's family may retain the stock interest. If the heirs have a majority interest, they may choose to become personally involved in management in order to receive income. Or they may choose to remain inactive, elect a new board of directors and force the company to pay dividends. In either case, the surviving stockholders may lose a voice in management and possibly their jobs, while the deceased's family may become heirs to a business on the brink of failure. If the heirs have a minority interest and are not employed by the surviving associates, their only means of receiving an income from the corporation will be through dividends.

After the death of a stockholder, the deceased's heirs or estate may offer to sell the stock interest to the surviving stockholders. Or an outside buyer may be interested in purchasing stock in the corporation. While all of the interested parties are alive, they can enter into a binding buy and sell agreement funded with life insurance. This is done with a stockholder's buy and sell agreement drawn up with the assistance of your corporate attorney and accountant.

Succession in a Limited Liability Company

A limited liability company is similar in structure to a partnership. Therefore, partners should provide for the contingency of another's death, incapacity or desire to sell equity in the partnership agreement or in a buy and sell agreement. In the absence of such an agreement, surviving partners have no right nor obligation to buy the deceased's partnership interest. If the surviving partner and deceased's heirs do nothing, the business is liquidated, resulting in auction price value for the salable assets.

Buy and sell agreements should be entered into while all partners are alive. The agreement will include a commitment by each partner not to dispose of his or her interest without first offering it at an agreed sale price to the partnership. The agreement will also include a provision for the partnership to buy a deceased partner's interest.

The purchase is usually funded from the proceeds of a life insurance policy written for that specific purpose.

Death of Key Employees

Many growing firms develop key employees who represent assets the firm cannot afford to be without. Even though these key employees may not own an interest in the firm, they are nonetheless valuable to its continuation. So what happens if a key employee dies?

Mail order businesses with key employees should consider life insurance payable to the firm on the death or disability of these people. How much life insurance? It should be an amount sufficient to offset financial losses during the readjustment period, to retain good credit standing and to assure customers and suppliers that the company will continue as usual. In addition, key-employee insurance could retire loans, mortgages, bonds, attract and train a successor or carry out ongoing plans for expansion and new developments. Talk to your insurance agent about the appropriate policy for insuring your business against the loss of a proprietor, a partner, a stockholder or a key employee. It's one of the costs of growth.

Enjoy Your Life

The primary reason you started your own business was to increase your opportunities to enjoy life. You wanted to offer a needed service, you wanted to help others, you wanted to extend your skills in mail order business and in business, you wanted to be able to afford the better things of life. However, you didn't want to spend your entire waking time working. In fact, you may get so caught up in the chase for success that you miss the opportunities that success brings along the way.

Those who have found success in the mail order business and other fields will tell you that success is often empty if not shared with others. And that doesn't mean waiting until a successful destination—say at $1 million net worth—is reached. It means sharing success with others along the way, on a day-to-day basis. Maybe, for you, this means sharing your success with your family, a few good friends or a charitable organization. In any case, consider that your financial success will mean much more to you if you can use it to bring physical, emotional or spiritual success to others.

Manage your life outside your business as you do your time at the business. Look for ways of helping others. Find methods of giving yourself the things you most enjoy, whether time with friends, time with hobbies, time with competitive sports, time alone or all of the above. Especially, take time to recharge your batteries. You will use lots of personal energy in starting, managing and growing your mail order business. Make sure you take the time to reenergize yourself.

When To Quit

The failure rate of new businesses is very high. It lowers as businesses mature. The longer you're in business, the greater the chance that you will continue in business. However, your mail order business can fail at any time, quite often due to poor recordkeeping. So a key element of continued success is maintaining good records and learning how to manage by them.

But there may come a time when business conditions require that you throw in the towel. If you're not making sufficient profit or are reducing your capital to losses, you will soon be in financial trouble. What to do?

First, cut overhead as much as possible. The sooner this is done, the longer your business will survive—maybe long enough to find a solution.

Next, sell unused or inefficient assets. Of course, you must maintain your working tools. But maybe you can move your office to a less expensive location—even back home.

Then talk with your creditors about the situation and what you plan to do. Some may be very helpful in offering a workable solution—an extension of credit, assistance in finding additional contracts or even purchase of stock in your business.

Finally, as necessary, talk with your attorney about your legal obligations and options. No one wants to declare bankruptcy, but it may be necessary. Or you may decide to set up a payment schedule for all debts and return to the work force as an employee.

There is no shame in failing to succeed—just in failing to try. If there are things you've learned from the experience, you can use them to increase your worth to an employer. Who better to manage a mail order business than one who has learned what doesn't work.

Of course, now that you've planned out how to minimize losses, you probably won't have to. In fact, you can look forward to retirement.

Planning To Retire

When should you retire from your profitable mail order business? When you want to. Some mail order business owners will hold off retiring until they are no longer physically able to work their trade. Others make plans to retire when they are 65 or even 62 years of age. Still others give their business 10 or 20 years to grow, then sell it to semiretire or move to a different trade. Some work their children into it, then gradually turn it over to them.

Some successful mail order business owners will sell their shares to a partner or to another corporation. Others will sell or give their equity in the business to a relative. Some will sell out to key employees or to competitors.

The business can be sold outright for cash, earning the owner a cash settlement for his or her equity. Or the seller can carry the paper or sell it on a contract with a down payment and monthly payments for a specified term. In this case, buyers will often require the seller to sign a noncompetition contract that says the seller can't go to work for a competing mail order business or start another mail order business in the same market.

Action Guidelines

This is the end of the beginning. You now have many of the tools you need to start and succeed with your own mail order business. Here's how you can put this final chapter into action:

✔ Apply the problem-solving techniques in this chapter to a current problem that your mail order business is facing or expects to face.

✔ Even if you don't plan to hire anyone, review the methods of managing employees. If nothing else, it will remind you of why you don't want to increase your staff for awhile.

✔ If you have or expect to hire employees, review the information on benefits programs to determine which best fit your business and philosophy.

✔ Find a local mailing service or noncompeting mail order business that may be able to help you during busy times.

✔ Consult with your insurance agent to make sure you are not undercovered nor overinsured.

✔ Plan today for how your business will survive the death of a principal, partner or key employee.

✔ Periodically review your expenses to ensure you are getting the most from each dollar you spend.

✔ Have fun with your mail order business and your life!

INDEX